SCOTTISH
COUNTRY RECIPES

COMPILED BY
PIPPA GOMAR & MOLLY PERHAM

RAVETTE BOOKS

Published by Ravette Books Limited
3 Glenside Estate, Star Road
Partridge Green, Horsham,
West Sussex RH13 8RA
(0403) 710392

Production: Oval Projects Ltd.
Cover design: Jim Wire
Typesetting: Artset Graphics
Printing & binding: Norhaven AS

All recipes are given in Imperial and Metric
weights and measures. Where measurements
are given in 'cups', these are American cups,
holding 8 fluid ounces.

The recipes contained in this book are traditional
and many have been compiled from archival sources.
Every effort has been made to ensure that the recipes
are correct.

Acknowledgements:

Mrs. Clunie for Brydon Tart, Apple Charlotte,
Lothian Gingerbread and Aberdeen Meat Roll.

Miss Bynner Griffiths for Crofter's Plum Pudding.

Mrs. Mary Bush for Cloutie Dumpling.

Mrs. Hammond for help and information.

RECIPES

SCOTLAND

Scotland is a rugged country with little more than a quarter of the land under cultivation. The soil is poorer than in England and the weather wetter and colder. In early times the mainstay of the Scottish peasant's diet used to be oats and barley, which grow well in the inhospitable climate. Every cottage had its own girnel, or oatmeal barrel, and oakcakes or bannocks were cooked on an iron bakestone over a peat fire. This method of cooking was used well into the last century in some of the Scottish Islands. For the modern Scottish housewife baked food still remain an important part of the diet, from freshly-baked morning rolls, or baps, to the substantial array of cakes, scones, gingerbread and shortbreads that are served for the favourite meal of the day — high tea.

Oats and barley were augmented by kail and by vegetables and fruits that grew wild in the hedgerows — raspberries, strawberries, gooseberries, blaeberries, wild spinach, carrots and nettles. The kail-pot was also made of iron — it was a large round cauldron with a lid and three legs that stood over the fire. Soups and broths, often substantial enough to be a meal on their own, were made from any available vegetables and bones of game, rabbit, meat or fish. The potato was introduced from Ireland in the 18th century, and at about that time knowledge of crop husbandry and improved methods of agriculture began to be used so that more varied vegetables were grown.

The uncultivated areas of Scotland, particularly in the North and West, are famous for their game. The rolling moorlands are home to red grouse, ptarmigan, blackcock, capercaillie, partridge, wild duck, pheasant, woodcock and snipe. Deer roam in the Highland forests.

The Scots have never eaten much pork, but Scottish beef and lamb have gained fame throughout the world. Traditional beef breeds include the Aberdeen Angus, the Galloway and the Highland. Cheviots and Shetlands are the most popular breeds of sheep.

The sheep and beef cattle graze on the uplands, while the lowlands provide rich pastureland for the dairy herds. The county of Ayrshire has given its name to a breed of cattle developed there that has become popular throughout Great Britain because of its high milk yield. Being high in butterfat, the milk is ideal for making cheese like Highland Soft. Dunlop, a hard cheese, is also made in this part of Scotland, as well as on the Orkneys, Arran and Islay. Scottish Cheddar is produced in creameries in the uplands.

Crowdie, an old Highland cheese, is made by souring milk naturally in the sun. The cream is then skimmed off for butter, and the thickened milk 'scrambled' on the stove to make the whey drain off. The resulting curds are wrapped in muslin and left to drain. Served with oat-cakes, crowdie has been eaten in the Highlands and Islands since the days of the Picts.

Fishing is an important Scottish industry, and has been so since the eleventh century. Until then, the Celtic Church had forbidden fish to be used as a food. Inland, the rivers of Scotland are stacked with salmon and trout, while huge catches of herring are landed at Aberdeen, and because they are so plentiful and cheap they have always been an important part of the Scottish diet — cooked in a large pot with tatties (potatoes) or fried in a coating of oatmeal. Those that were not consumed by the local people were preserved by salting and smoking. Scotch herring are ideal for kippers because they are large and have a high fat content. Loch Fyne remains the centre of the kipper trade.

Other fish caught off Scottish shores are haddock, cod mackerel, halibut, sole and plaice. Finnan haddock is a particular delicacy that originated in the village of Findon near Aberdeen. Smokies, or "pinwiddies" are small haddock that have been hot-smoked, and these come from the tiny hamlet of Auchmithie near Arbroath.

Scottish traditional cuisine tends to be heavy and filling to satisfy the appetites of men who have spent a day out in the cold. But it also owes a rather more delicate touch to the influence of the French, who came and went during the period of the Auld Alliance in the 16th century. James V of Scotland married a French noblewoman, Mary of Lorraine, and entertaining in the French manner became the rage amongst the aristocracy. The French influence is still evident in some of the recipes and culinary terms, but good, plain, wholesome food is what the country has always been, and still is, famous for.

Fair fa' your honest, sonsie face,
Great chieftain o' the puddin'-race
Aboon them a' ye tak your place,
Painch, tripe, or thairm:
Weel are ye wordy o'a grace
As lang's my arm.

From *To A Haggis* by Robert Burns.

HIGHLAND GAME SOUP

Serves 6-8

This rich, clear soup from the Highlands of Scotland can be made with left-over trimmings and carcasses from any type of game — grouse, pheasant or partridge; rabbit, hare or venison.

Left-over trimmings and carcasses of game
1 onion
1 carrot
1 blade of mace
1 bay leaf
3 cloves
2 sprigs of parsley
2 pints (1.15 litres) beef stock
Salt and pepper
1 oz (25 g) lean beef
1 glass Marsala or sherry

Put the left-over trimmings and carcasses into a large saucepan.

Add the peeled and sliced onion and carrot, the mace, bay leaf, cloves and parsley.

Pour over the beef stock.

Season with salt and pepper.

Bring to the boil.

Skim off any scum that rises to the surface.

Simmer for two hours, then strain.

Return the soup to the saucepan and add the beef, coarsely chopped.

Bring to the boil again and strain.

Add the Marsala or sherry and reheat before serving.

LORRAINE SOUP

This delicately-flavoured soup owes its origin to the French influence in Scotland. The name comes from Mary of Lorraine, the wife of James V of Scotland, and mother of Mary, Queen of Scots.

1 lb (450 g) cooked white meat — chicken, rabbit or veal
2 oz (50 g) blanched almonds
2 hard-boiled egg yolks
1 tablespoon fine white breadcrumbs
3 pints (1.75 litres) good white stock
Salt and pepper
A pinch of powdered mace
1 teaspoon lemon juice
¼ pint (150 ml/⅔ cup) cream
1 tablespoon chopped parsley

Mince the meat finely.

Add the almonds and egg yolks and mix with the meat in a liquidizer.

Heat the crumbs in a little of the stock and add to the liquidizer.

Put the liquidized ingredients and the rest of the stock into a saucepan.

Season with salt, pepper, mace and lemon juice.

Bring to the boil.

Remove from the heat and stir in the cream.

Reheat gently, but do not allow to boil.

Serve hot, garnished with chopped parsley.

SCOTCH BROTH

Serves 6-8

This soup is so nourishing and filling that it is a meal in itself. It has always been popular with farming families.

1 lb (450 g) neck of mutton
4 pints (2.25 litres) cold water
2 oz (50 g) pearl barley, washed
2 oz (50 g) dried peas, soaked overnight
2 carrots
2 leeks
1 small turnip
1 onion
1 stick celery
Salt and pepper
Half a small cabbage, shredded
A sprig of parsley

Put the meat into a large saucepan.

Cover with cold water.

Add the salt, pearl barley, and peas.

Bring to the boil.

Skim off any scum that rises to the surface.

Dice the carrots, leeks, turnip, onion and celery and add to the pan.

Season with salt and pepper.

Bring to the boil, cover, and simmer for 2½ hours.

Add the shredded cabbage and cook for a further 20 minutes.

Adjust the seasoning.

Garnish with chopped parsley before serving.

FEATHER FOWLIE

1 roasting chicken
2 oz (50 g) lean ham
1 onion, peeled and sliced
1 stick of celery, chopped
1 carrot, sliced
A sprig each of parsley and thyme
1 blade of mace
3 pints (1.75 litres) cold water
3 egg yolks, beaten
2 tablespoons warmed cream
Salt
Chopped parsley for garnishing

Skin and joint the chicken.

Soak the joints in cold salted water for 30 minutes.

Drain the joints and rinse them under running water.

Put the joints, ham, prepared vegetables and herbs into a large saucepan.

Pour over the cold water.

Cover and bring to the boil.

Skim off any scum that rises to the surface.

Simmer gently for 1½-2 hours until the chicken is tender.

Strain the stock into a basin.

Allow to cool, then remove all the grease.

Return the stock to a clean pan and bring very slowly to the boil.

Simmer gently, uncovered, for 15 minutes.

Remove the pan from the heat and gradually stir in the beaten egg yolks and warmed cream.

Heat to cook the eggs slightly, but do not allow to boil.

Mince a little of the cooked chicken breast and add to the soup. (The rest of the meat can be served as a second course, or saved for later use.)

Add salt to taste. Garnish with chopped parsley.

COCK-A-LEEKIE   Serves 6-8

This is traditionally served as the first course on Hogmanay or at a Burn's Supper. The Scots so love their national soup that many odes have been written to it.

> 'Lang may ye live, an' lang enjoy
> Ilk blessin' life can gie,
> Health, wealth, content and pleasure,
> An' cock-a-leekie.'

1 boiling fowl, with giblets
4 pints (2.25 litres) cold water
6 shredded leeks
2 tablespoons rice
1 tablespoon chopped parsley
Salt and pepper to taste

Place the fowl and giblets in a large saucepan and cover with cold water.

Bring to the boil. Skim off any scum.

Simmer gently for 2 hours, skimming again if necessary.

Add the shredded leeks and rice and simmer for a further hour.

Remove the bird and giblets from the soup.

Add the chopped parsley. Season to taste.

The chicken meat can be served as a separate course.

HOTCH POTCH .

Also called Hairst Bree, meaning harvest browth, this soup-stew was made in the summer when all the vegetables were young and crisp. The freshness of the vegetables gives the soup its sweet flavour.

> 'Then here's to ilka kindly Scot:
> Wi' mony gude broths he boils his pot,
> But rare hotch-potch beats a' the lot,
> It smells and smacks sae brawly.'

Sheriff Bell

8 oz (225 g) neck of lamb
2 pints (1.15 litres) water
Salt and pepper
3 fresh young carrots
2 fresh young turnips
½ small cauliflower
1 onion (or 4 spring onions)
4 oz (100 g) broad beans
4 oz (100 g) shelled peas
4 leaves of lettuce or cabbage
1 level teaspoon sugar
1 tablespoon chopped parsley

Put the meat into a saucepan and cover with the cold water.

Season with salt and pepper.

Bring to the boil.

Skim off any scum that rises to the surface.

Simmer gently for 1½ hours.

Dice the carrots and turnips.

Divide the cauliflower into small sprigs.

Peel and slice the onion or spring onions.

Add these and the broad beans to the saucepan and simmer for a further 30-40 minutes.

Add the shelled peas and shredded lettuce or cabbage leaves and simmer for a further 10 minutes.

Remove the meat and cut it into small dice.

Return to the pan.

Add the sugar and chopped parsley.

Check the seasoning.

Serve hot.

LENTIL BRO   Serves 8-10

This soup comes from the Shetland Islands.

2 oz (50 g) butter
8 oz (225 g) lentils
2 oz (50 g) barley
1 large onion, finely chopped
1 carrot, diced
2 sticks of celery, chopped
½ small turnip, diced
Salt and pepper
4 pints (2.25 litres) ham stock
Chopped parsley for garnishing

Melt the butter in a large saucepan.

Add the lentils, barley, and prepared vegetables.

Season with salt and pepper.

Cook gently for 10 minutes, stirring occasionally.

Add the stock.

Bring to the boil and simmer for 1½-2 hours.

Check the seasoning.

Serve hot, garnished with chopped parsley.

PARTAN BREE

Serves 6-8

Partan is the Gaelic name for crab, and bree means liquid or gravy.

1 large cooked crab (weighing about 2-3 lbs/1-1.5 kg)
2 oz (50 g) rice
1 pint (600 ml/2½ cups) milk
1 pint (600 ml/2½ cups) water
¼ pint (150 ml ⅔ cup) single cream
Anchovy essence
Salt and pepper
Chopped parsley for garnish

Remove all the meat from the crab, keeping the claw meat separate.

Put the rice in a saucepan with the milk and water and cook until tender.

Put the cooked rice with some of the cooking liquid into a liquidizer.

Add the crab meat, except the meat from the claws.

Liquidize until you have a fine purée.

Spoon the purée back into the cooking liquid.

Add the cream and anchovy essence to taste.

Season with salt and pepper.

Add the claw meat and heat through gently, but do not boil.

Serve hot, garnished with chopped parsley.

CULLEN SKINK

Serves 4

This is a traditional fisherman's soup from the North East of Scotland. It should be made with a true Finnan-haddie — a Finnan haddock that has been lightly smoked but not dyed. Skink is an old Scots word for soup or broth.

1 large smoked Finnan haddock
1 onion, chopped
½ pint (300 ml/1½ cups) water
Salt and pepper
1 pint (600 ml/2½ cups) milk
1 oz (25 g) butter
½ lb (225 g) mashed potato

Put the haddock and chopped onion into a saucepan and cover with water.

Bring to the boil and simmer for about 15 minutes, until the flesh comes away from the bone.

Put the flesh to one side.

Put the skin and bones back into the pan.

Season with salt and pepper.

Cook for a further hour.

Strain the fish stock and discard the skin and bones.

Add the flaked flesh, milk, butter and mashed potato to the fish stock.

Bring back to the boil and simmer for a few minutes.

Serve hot.

ANGUS FISH SOUP

Soups and broths made from left-over fish bones and heads are typical examples of Scottish thriftiness. This particular soup is thickened with egg and cream, which suggests a French influence. In the Middle Ages, French monks settled in the area in large numbers.

6 fresh haddock heads
2 pints (1.15 litres) water
1 carrot
1 stick of celery
Half a small turnip
3-4 sprigs parsley
Salt and pepper
2 oz (50g) butter
2 oz (50g) flour
½ pint (300 ml/1¼ cups) milk
1 egg yolk
3 tablespoons double cream
1 tablespoon chopped parsley

Rinse the fish heads and put them into a saucepan with the water.

Bring to the boil.

Skim off any scum that rises to the surface.

Add the vegetables and parsley.

Season with salt and pepper.

Simmer until the vegetables are tender.

Strain.

Melt the butter in a clean saucepan.

Gradually stir in the flour and cook gently for a couple of minutes.

Remove the pan from the heat and gradually stir in the strained broth.

Stir in the milk.

Return to the heat, bring to the boil and simmer for a couple of minutes.

Blend the egg yolk and cream together and add to the soup.

Do not allow to boil.

Serve hot, garnished with chopped parsley.

KAIL BROSE   Serves 6-8

There are dozens of different recipes for this dish, but the basic ingredients are curly kail cooked in water or stock, thickened with oatmeal, barley or rice. It used to be a staple food in Scotland.

> 'When I see our Scots lads,
> Wi' their kilts and cockades,
> That sae aften hae lounder'd our foes, man;
> I think to mysel',
> On the meal and the yill,
> And the fruits o'our Scottish kail brose, man.'
>   *A Cogie o' Yill* by Andrew Shirrefs (1762-1800)

1 lb (450 g) green curly kail
3 pints (1.75 litres) stock
Salt and pepper
1 oz (25 g) barley or 2 oz (50 g) oatmeal

Cook the barley or oatmeal in the stock for half an hour.

Wash and shred the kail and add to the stock.

Cook for another half hour.

Season with salt and pepper.

Serve hot with oatcakes.

BAKED STUFFED HERRINGS — Serves 4

4 herrings

For the stuffing:
1 small onion
2 mushrooms
½ cup stale breadcrumbs
1 large soft roe
½ teaspoon mixed herbs
1 teaspoon chopped parsley
1 teaspoon softened butter
Salt and pepper

Remove the heads of the fish. Clean and wash thoroughly.

Split open and remove the backbones.

Remove the roes, reserving one for the stuffing.

To make the stuffing:
Chop the onion and mushrooms finely.

Mix with the breadcrumbs, roe, herbs, parsley, and softened butter. Season with salt and pepper.

Divide the stuffing into four equal portions.

Spread a portion over each herring.

Roll up carefully and tie securely with thread.

Place the herrings in a greased pie dish. Dot with butter.

Cover with greaseproof paper.

Bake in a moderately hot over for 35 minutes.

Remove the paper and allow to brown.

Remove the thread before serving.

Serve with chips, mustard sauce, and a green salad.

Oven: 375°F/190°C   Gas Mark 5

HERRINGS IN OATMEAL

Serves 4

4 large herrings
Salt and pepper
4 oz (100 g) oatmeal
2 oz (50 g) butter
1 tablespoon oil
Lemon to garnish

Wash and gut the herrings.

Split them.

Run the blade of a knife down the backbone, pressing firmly, and lift it out.

Sprinkle the herrings with salt and pepper.

Dip the fish in the oatmeal, pressing it well in until they are well coated.

Heat the butter and oil in a frying pan, but do not allow the pan to get too hot, or the oatmeal will burn and the fish become too dry.

Fry the herrings, split side down, for about 4 minutes or until well browned.

Turn and fry the other side until brown and crisp.

Drain on kitchen paper.

Garnish with lemon wedges.

PICKLED HERRINGS

6 fresh herrings with roes
Salt and pepper
Butter
1 large onion
2 whole cloves
6 whole peppercorns
1 bay leaf
¼ pint (150 ml/⅔ cup) white vinegar
¼ pint (150 ml/⅔ cup) water

Clean the herrings.

Cut in half lengthwise, remove the bones and clean the insides.

Season with salt and pepper.

Roll up each fillet with the skin on the outside.

Brush an ovenproof dish with melted butter.

Arrange the herring rolls alternately with the roes in the dish.

Peel and slice the onion.

Arrange on top of the fish.

Add the cloves, peppercorns and bay leaf.

Mix the vinegar and water together and pour over the fish.

Cover the dish and bake in a cool oven for 1 hour.

Remove the covering and bake for a further 20 minutes.

Leave to cool.

Serve cold with potato salad.

Oven: 300°F/150°C   Gas Mark 2

FINNAN HADDOCK

The Finnan, or Findon, haddock takes its name from a village in Kincardineshire. It is split and cleaned before curing, and is a golden yellow colour with a nutty flavour. Finnan haddocks may be grilled, steamed, or poached.

To grill: Brush each haddock with melted butter and grill lightly on both sides. Top each haddock with two lightly poached eggs.

To steam: Cut each haddock lengthwise, then across. Place in a saucepan with enough water to cover. Add a rasher of bacon. Cover with a close-fitting lid and steam for 5 minutes.

To poach: Cut each haddock in half down the middle. Put into a large saucepan and cover with boiling water. Simmer gently for 5 minutes. Drain off the water.

To make a sauce for poached Finnan haddock:

½ oz (15 g) butter
1 teaspoon cornflour
½ pint (300 ml/1¼ cups) milk
Salt and pepper
1 hard-boiled egg
1 teaspoon chopped parsley

Melt the butter in a small saucepan.

Cream the cornflour with a little of the milk.

Add to the melted butter.

Stir in the remainder of the milk.

Bring to the boil, stirring all the time.

Season with salt and pepper.

Pour over the fish.

Chop the hard-boiled egg and sprinkle on top.

Garnish with chopped parsley.

CRAPPIT HEIDS

This recipe comes from the Hebrides, and is a way of using up the liver from white fish. The liver melts away into the oatmeal when it is cooked, and the bones from the head add flavour. The Scots word 'crap' means to stuff or fill.

4 large haddock heads
4 haddock livers
Oatmeal
Salt and pepper
Milk to bind

Clean the fish heads thoroughly.

Place the fish livers in a bowl and cover with cold water.

Add some salt and soak for 1 hour.

Strain.

Chop the livers and mix with an equal quantity of oatmeal.

Season with salt and pepper.

Moisten with a little milk.

Stuff the haddock heads loosely with the filling, leaving room for the oatmeal to swell.

Tie securely with thread.

Wrap in foil and put into a pan of boiling water.

Simmer for 30 minutes.

Serve the heads on their own or with portions of plain boiled fish.

GRILLED MACKEREL WITH GOOSEBERRY SAUCE

Serves 4

The sharp flavour of a gooseberry sauce goes well with the oiliness of mackerel.

4 medium mackerel
A little melted butter
Salt and pepper

For the sauce:
8 oz (225 g) gooseberries
½ oz (15 g) butter
1 oz (25 g) sugar
A pinch of ground nutmeg
1 teaspoon lemon juice
Salt and pepper

Ask the fishmonger to gut the mackerel.

Wash the fish thoroughly and with a sharp knife make three diagonal scores on each side.

Brush with melted butter.

Sprinkle with salt and pepper.

Put the mackerel into a buttered grill pan and grill slowly for about 10 minutes on each side.

To make the sauce:

Top and tail the gooseberries and wash them.

Put into a saucepan with the butter and cook gently to a soft pulp.

Rub the fruit through a sieve.

Stir in the sugar, nutmeg, lemon juice, and a little salt and pepper.

Serve with the grilled mackerel.

BAKED STUFFED MACKEREL

Serves 4

4 medium-sized mackerel
4 oz (100 g) fresh white breadcrumbs
1 dessertspoon chopped parsley
2 spring onions, finely chopped
Salt and pepper
Melted butter

Clean and fillet the mackerel.

Lay four fillets in a buttered ovenproof dish, insides uppermost.

Mix the breadcrumbs with the parsley and chopped spring onions.

Season with salt and pepper.

Stir in enough melted butter to make a paste.

Spread the paste over the fillets in the dish.

Lay the other four fillets on top, inside downwards, and press them together.

Cover with greaseproof paper.

Bake in a moderate oven for 30 minutes.

Oven: 350°F/180°C   Gas Mark 4

FILLETS OF SOLE

Serves 6

This recipe comes from the Duart Bay district of Argyll, off the Sound of Mull.

6 fillets of sole, weighing about 6 oz (175 g) each
1 oz (25 g) butter
12 oz (350 g) button mushrooms
Salt and pepper
¼ pint (150 ml/⅔ cup) water
½ pint (300 ml/1¼ cups) fish stock
2 egg yolks
2 tablespoons double cream

Wipe the fillets.

Butter an ovenproof dish and cover the base with half the mushrooms. Lay the fillets on top.

Cover with the remaining mushrooms.

Season with salt and pepper and dot with butter.

Pour over the water.

Cover with buttered paper and bake in a moderate oven for about 10 minutes, or until cooked.

Put the fillets and mushrooms on to a serving dish and keep warm.

Pour the cooking liquid into a saucepan and bring to the boil.

Simmer until the liquid has reduced to a glaze, then add the fish stock and simmer for a further 3-4 minutes.

Remove from the heat and blend in the egg yolks lightly beaten with the cream.

Reheat the sauce, but do not allow to boil.

Pour the sauce over the fillets and serve.

Oven: 350°F/180°C   Gas Mark 4.

NEWHAVEN CREAM

This baked fish pudding gets its name from an old fishing village near Edinburgh. It may also be steamed in a bowl for about 1½ hours, instead of baking in the oven.

1 lb (450 g) Aberdeen fish fillet
½ pint (300 ml/1¼ cups) milk
2 oz (50 g) melted butter
3 oz (75 g) fresh white breadcrumbs
2 tablespoons chopped parsley
3 eggs
¼ pint (150 ml/⅔ cup) cream
Salt and pepper

For the sauce:
¼ pint (150 ml/⅔ cup) milk
½ oz (15 g) butter
½ oz (15 g) flour
1 tablespoon chopped parsley

Put the fish into a saucepan. Pour over the milk.

Bring to the boil, cover and simmer for 5 minutes.

Skin and flake the fish. Reserve the cooking liquid.

Put the melted butter, breadcrumbs, parsley, eggs and cream into a bowl and add the fish.

Mix together thoroughly. Season with salt and pepper.

Pour into a greased 2 pint (1 litre) soufflé mould.

Cover with greaseproof paper or foil.

Set the dish in a tin containing about 1 inch (2.5 cm) water and bake in a moderate oven for 30 minutes.

To make the sauce:

Melt the butter in a small saucepan and add the flour.

Cook gently for a couple of minutes, then gradually add the milk, stirring all the time to prevent lumps.

Bring to the boil so that the sauce thickens.

Season and add the parsley.

To serve:

Turn the fish pudding out on to a warm serving dish and pour over the sauce. Serve hot.

Oven: 350°F/180°C   Gas Mark 4

TROUT WITH ALMONDS   Serves 4

4 rainbow trout
1 oz (25 g) seasoned flour
3 oz (75 g) butter
1 tablespoon corn oil
2 oz (50 g) flaked almonds
Juice of half a lemon

Clean the fish but leave the heads on.

Wash and dry the fish thoroughly.

Toss in the seasoned flour.

Melt 1 oz (25 g) of the butter and the oil in a frying pan.

Fry the fish two at a time for 5 minutes on each side.

Drain and keep warm on a serving dish.

Wipe the frying pan clean and melt the rest of the butter.

Fry the almonds until they are brown.

Remove the pan from the heat and stir in the lemon juice.

Spoon the almond mixture over the fish and serve.

COLD SALMON MAYONNAISE

This makes an ideal centrepiece for a buffet dinner.

1 large salmon — weighing about 4½ lbs (2 kg)
¼ pint (150 ml/⅔ cup) white wine
A bouquet garni
1 packet aspic jelly
Cucumber, radishes, hard-boiled egg, etc. to garnish

For the mayonnaise:
2 egg yolks
½ pint (300 ml/1¼ cups) olive oil
Salt and pepper
½ teaspoon Dijon mustard
Lemon juice

Wash the salmon thoroughly.

Half fill a fish kettle or large pan with water.

Add the wine and bouquet garni.

Bring to the boil.

Lower in the salmon carefully.

Simmer gently, allowing 10 minutes per lb.

Leave the fish to cool in the water.

When cool, remove the skin.

Lift out carefully on to a serving dish.

Following the instructions on the packet, coat the salmon with aspic.

Garnish with sliced cucumber, radishes, hard-boiled egg, etc.

Serve with mayonnaise and salad vegetables.

To make the mayonnaise:

Make sure that the egg yolks and olive oil are at room temperature.

Put the egg yolks into a bowl, and add some salt, pepper and the mustard.

Use a wooden spoon to stir the ingredients to a smooth paste.

Blend in a few drops of lemon juice, and then start adding the olive oil very gradually, drop by drop.

Stir steadily until all the oil has been absorbed.

Check the seasoning and add a little more lemon juice to sharpen the flavour.

GRILLED SALMON STEAKS   Serves 4

4 slices of salmon, about ¾ inch (1.5 cm) thick
Butter
Salt and pepper
Sliced lemon and sprigs of parsley for garnish

Wipe the salmon steaks with a damp cloth.

Brush over with a little melted butter.

Season with salt and pepper.

Cook under a hot grill for 6-8 minutes on each side.

Place on a serving dish and garnish with slices of lemon and sprigs of parsley.

TWEED KETTLE

The Tweed is one of the great salmon rivers of Scotland. This recipe comes from Edinburgh.

2 lbs (900 g) fresh salmon
2 spring onions, finely chopped
A pinch of mace
¼ pint (150 ml/⅔ cup) dry white wine
Salt and pepper
1 oz (25 g) butter
4 oz (100 g) mushrooms
1 tablespoon chopped parsley

Put the salmon into a fish kettle or large pan and cover with water.

Bring to the boil, simmer gently for 3 minutes.

Remove the skin from the salmon and take out all the bones.

Cut the flesh into small cubes.

Return the skin and bones to the cooking liquid, bring to the boil and simmer for 15 minutes.

Strain and pour off ¼ pint (150 ml/⅔ cup) into a clean saucepan.

Add the cubed fish, chopped spring onions, mace, and white wine. Season with salt and pepper.

Cover and simmer gently for 10 minutes.

Melt the butter in another saucepan.

Chop the mushrooms into small pieces and cook them gently in the butter.

Drain, and add to the salmon mixture.

Continue cooking the mixture for a further 5 minutes. Turn out on to a serving dish garnish with chopped parsley.

STOVED CHICKEN

This popular chicken dish from the Highlands also has a French influence. The French word *étouffée* means stewed in a closed vessel.

1 chicken, weighing about 3 lbs (1.5 kg)
2 oz (50 g) butter
2 lbs (900 g) potatoes
2 onions
Salt and pepper
1 pint (600 ml/2½ cups) chicken stock
Chopped parsley to garnish

Joint the chicken into eight pieces.

Melt half the butter in a frying pan and lightly brown the chicken joints.

Peel and slice the potatoes and onions.

Grease a casserole dish.

Place a layer of potato slices on the bottom, followed by a layer of onion.

Season well with salt and pepper.

Arrange four pieces of chicken on top.

Dot with some of the remaining butter.

Continue the layers until all the ingredients are used up, ending with a layer of potatoes.

Pour over the stock.

Cover with a piece of buttered greaseproof paper.

Put on the lid.

Cook in a cool oven for 2½ hours.

Sprinkle with chopped parsley before serving.

Oven: 300°F/150°C   Gas Mark 2

HOWTOWDIE WITH DRAPPIT EGGS

Serves 6

This dish of stewed chicken has a strong French influence. The name is thought to come from the Old French *hutaudeau*, meaning a young chicken. Drappit eggs are poached eggs. The cooked bird was placed on a nest of spinach, surrounded by the eggs. The chicken is stuffed with skirlie — a mixture of oatmeal, suet and spices. Skirlie used to be a meal in itself, when there was little else to eat.

1 roasting chicken, weighing about 3 lbs (1.5 kg)
2 oz (50 g) butter
8 baby onions
2 whole cloves
6 peppercorns
3 allspice berries
Salt
1 pint (600 ml/2½ cups) chicken stock
2 lbs (900 g) spinach
A little cream or butter
1 chicken liver, finely chopped
6 eggs

For the skirlie (stuffing):
2 oz (50 g) shredded suet
2 onions, finely chopped
4 oz (100 g) oatmeal
½ teaspoon mace
½ teaspoon ground coriander
A pinch of nutmeg
Salt and pepper

To make the skirlie:

Heat the suet in a frying pan.

Add the onions and cook until soft and slightly browned.

Add the oatmeal and spices.

Season well with salt and pepper.

Fry until the oatmeal is brown and crunchy.

To cook the chicken:

Stuff the chicken with the skirlie.

Truss securely.

Melt the butter in a large, flameproof casserole.

Add the whole baby onions and cook gently until soft.

Put in the chicken and brown on all sides.

Add the cloves, peppercorns, allspice berries, salt and stock.

Bring to the boil.

Cover the dish and put into a moderate oven for 1½ hours, or until the chicken is tender.

Meanwhile prepare and cook the spinach.

Purée the spinach and beat in a little thick cream or butter.

When the chicken is cooked remove it from the casserole and place on a warmed serving dish.

Strain the stock into a saucepan, add the chopped chicken liver and bring to the boil.

Poach the eggs in the stock.

To serve:

Arrange a nest of spinach around the chicken with the poached eggs on top.

Serve the chicken gravy separately in a sauceboat.

ROAST GROUSE

Serves 4

The season for grouse is 12 August to 10 December. There are four types of grouse — red, black, white (ptarmigan) and wood grouse (capercaillie). The red grouse is considered to be the best. Grouse need to be hung for at least a week before eating.

2 young grouse, weighing just over 1 lb (450 g) each
2 oz (50 g) butter
Juice of 1 lemon
4 oz (100 g) cranberries or whortleberries
Salt and pepper
4 rashers of streaky beacon
Livers from the grouse
2 slices of toast
Watercress for garnish

Wipe the insides of the birds.

Soften the butter and mix with the berries and lemon juice.

Season with salt and pepper.

Put half the mixture inside each bird.

Lay two rashers of bacon over the breast of each bird.

Put into a roasting tin and cover with foil.

Roast in a moderately hot oven for 30 minutes.

Meanwhile cook the grouse livers in boiling water or stock for 3 minutes.

Reserve the stock and mash the livers with a little butter and season with salt and pepper.

Spread on the slices of toast.

Take the grouse from the oven and remove the foil.

Place the birds on the slices of toast.

Return to the oven and roast for a further 15 minutes, basting occasionally with the pan juices.

Place the grouse on a warmed serving dish.

Pour off any fat from the roasting tin, and add the reserved liver stock to the pan juices.

Bring to the boil, and season.

Garnish the grouse with watercress.

Serve with the gravy, game chips, redcurrant jelly and bread sauce.

Oven: 400°F/200°C   Gas Mark 6.

ROAST PHEASANT

Serves 6

The pheasant season is from 1st October to 1st February, and they are in prime condition in November and December. Pheasant are often bought by the brace — which means a cock and a hen bird. The cock usually weighs 3-3¼ lb (1.5-1.6 kg), and the hen bird about 2-2½ lb (1-1.5 kg). The hen bird usually has more flavour and is less dry than the cock. Birds should be hung for at least ten days.

A brace of pheasant
6 oz (175 g) fresh white breadcrumbs
4 oz (100 g) melted butter
4 rashers of streaky bacon
Watercress for garnish

Wipe the birds inside and out.

Stir the breadcrumbs into the melted butter.

Divide the stuffing mixture into two and spoon into the carcass of each bird.

Truss the birds and place in a roasting tin.

Lay two rashers of bacon over the breast of each bird.

Roast in a hot oven for 10 minutes, then reduce the heat and cook for a further 45 minutes.

Ten minutes before the end of cooking time remove the bacon so that the breasts can brown.

Arrange the roast birds on a serving dish and garnish with watercress.

Serve with game chips and bread sauce.

Oven: 425°F/220°C   Gas Mark 7
Reduce to: 350°F/180°G gas Mark 4

PIGEON CASSEROLE

Serves 4

During the 19th century most large houses had a dovecot and pigeons were a source of extra meat.

2 pigeons
1 oz (25 g) butter
1 tablespoon cooking oil
4 oz (100 g) streaky bacon
2 onions, peeled and sliced
½ pint (300 ml/1¼ cups) tomato juice
½ pint (300 ml/1¼ cups) chicken stock
A bouquet garni
Salt and pepper
2 slices white bread
A little lard

Wipe the pigeons, and cut each one in half along the breast and backbone.

Heat the butter and oil in a frying pan until smoking hot and brown the pigeon pieces all over.

Transfer to a casserole dish.

Cut the bacon into pieces and fry with the onion in the remaining fat. Transfer to a casserole dish.

Pour over the tomato juice and stock, add the bouquet garni, and season with salt and pepper.

Cover the casserole and bake in a moderately hot oven for 2 hours, or until the meat is tender.

Near the end of cooking time cut the crusts off the bread and cut each slice into four triangles.

Heat the lard in a frying pan and fry the pieces of bread until they are golden brown on each side.

Remove the casserole from the oven, take out the bouquet garni and scatter the triangles of bread over the surface.

Oven: 375°F/190°C   Gas Mark 5.

SUTHERLAND VENISON

3-4 lb (1.5-1.75 kg) haunch of red deer, boned
Salt and pepper
2 oz (50 g) butter

For the suet crust pastry:
2 lbs (900 g) self-raising flour
1 lb (450 g) shredded suet
Salt and pepper
Cold water to mix

Season the meat well with salt and pepper.

Melt the butter in a large roasting tin with a grid in the bottom.

To make the pastry, sift the flour into a large mixing bowl. Add salt and pepper.

Add the suet, and enough cold water to make a firm dough. Turn out on to a floured pastry board.

Roll out the pastry into a large circle about ½ inch (1 cm) thick.

Lay the meat in the centre and wrap the pastry around it.

Seal the joints with water and press firmly together.

Place on the grid in a roasting tin and roast in a moderate oven for 20 minutes per lb (450 g), ocassionally basting the top with butter.

When cooked, remove from the oven and leave in a warm place for 15 minutes to let the juices settle.

Season the pan juices and pour into a sauceboat to serve with the meat.

Cut the pastry off the meat.

Carve the meat and serve with pieces of the pastry and redcurrant jelly.

Oven: 350°F/180°C   Gas Mark 4

CIVET OF VENISON

1½ lbs (675 g) venison
2 rashers of bacon
Seasoned flour
1 oz (35 g) lard
1 oz (25 g) flour
1 tablespoon wine vinegar
1 glass red wine or port
¼ pint (150 ml/⅔ cup) stock
2 onions, sliced
2 oz (25 g) mushrooms, sliced
Pepper

Cut the venison meat into cubes.

Remove the rind from the bacon and cut into pieces.

Toss the venison and bacon in seasoned flour.

Melt the lard in a large saucepan and fry the venison and bacon until brown all over.

Sprinkle over the flour, stir, and cook gently for 2 minutes.

Gradually add the vinegar, red wine, and stock, stirring all the time to prevent lumps.

Add the sliced onions.

Season with pepper to taste.

Cover with a well-fitting lid and simmer for 2-2½ hours until tender.

Add the sliced mushrooms 30 minutes before the end of cooking time.

BRAISED HAUNCH OF VENISON   Serves 8

Red deer are the most common in the Highlands, and they are now being farmed commercially in the Grampians. The stag season is from 1st July to 20th October, and the hind season from 21st October to 15th February. Hind meat has less fat and less flavour than stag, and the joints are smaller. There are also roe and fallow deer, but these are less numerous. The meat should hang for two to three weeks before use. Marinating for a couple of days before cooking makes it more tender.

4 lb (1.75 kg) haunch of venison
2 oz (50 g) lard
2 onions
2 carrots
4 sticks of celery
1 orange
1 pint (600 ml/2½ cups) stock
1 teaspoon salt
2 tablespoons redcurrant or cranberry jelly
1 oz (25 g) butter
1 oz (25 g) flour

For the marinade:
4 glasses red wine
2 tablespoons oil
2 sliced onions
1 bay leaf
6 large black peppercorns
10 juniper berries
A sprig of parsley

Tie the meat into shape and put into a deep dish.

Put all the marinade ingredients into a saucepan and heat to boiling point.

Leave to cool.

Pour the cool marinade over the meat and leave for two days, turning once or twice.

When ready to cook, drain off the marinade and reserve it.

Dry the meat with a paper towel.

Melt the lard in a fireproof casserole and brown the meat on all sides.

Remove from the casserole and put in the sliced vegetables and strips of orange peel.

Cover and cook gently for 10 minutes.

Lay the joint of meat on the bed of vegetables.

Add the marinade liquid, the stock, and salt.

Bring to the boil.

Transfer to a moderate oven for 3 hours, or until the meat is tender.

Remove the meat to a heated serving dish.

Strain the stock from the vegetables and arrange them around the meat.

Put the stock into a saucepan and add the juice of the orange and the jelly.

Work the butter and flour together until they form a smooth paste.

Break off little pieces and add to the stock to thicken it.

Whisk with a fork so that they are well blended and the gravy is smooth.

Serve gravy around the meat or separately in a sauceboat.

Oven: 350°F/180°C   Gas Mark 4

HAGGIS

Haggis is generally considered to be the national dish of Scotland. It is a simple, frugal meal using those parts of an animal that might otherwise be discarded, mixed with oats and seasonings.

Haggis is eaten throughout the year, but particularly on Hogmanay (31 December) and on Burns' Night (25 January). At Burns' suppers an elaborate ritual called the 'Ceremony of the Piping of the Haggis' is performed. The haggis is carried in on a silver platter to the sound of bagpipes. While the host quotes Burns' *Address to a Haggis,* it is slashed open with a *skein dhu* the small dagger traditionally worn in the Scotsman's knee-length sock. The haggis is then piped back to the kitchen, where it is dished out with chappit tatties and bashed neeps (hot mashed potatoes and swedes). It is usual to serve small glasses of neat whisky with the haggis — this is sipped in between mouthfuls, or poured over the haggis.

The stomach bag and pluck (heart, liver and lights)
   of a sheep
3 onions
1 lb (450 g) pinhead oatmeal
8 oz (225 g) shredded suet
Salt and pepper

Wash the stomach bag thoroughly in cold water.

Turn it inside out and scald it.

Scrape the surface with a knife.

Soak overnight in cold salted water.

Next day wash the pluck (heart, liver and lights) and put them into a pan of boiling water, letting the windpipe hang over the side.

Add a teaspoon of salt.

Boil for 2 hours.

Remove the pluck from the pan and cut away the windpipe and any gristle.

Parboil the onions, drain them and reserve the water.

Chop the onions thoroughly.

Toast the pinhead oatmeal until golden brown.

Mince half the liver with all the heart and lights.

Stir in the chopped onions, toasted oatmeal and shredded suet.

Season well with salt and pepper.

Add enough of the water from boiling the onions to make a soft mixture.

With the rough surface of the stomach bag on the outside, fill it three-quarters full with the mixture — room must be left for the oatmeal to swell.

Sew the bag up with a trussing needle using coarse thread or very fine string.

Prick the bag here and there with the needle.

Place the haggis on an old enamel plate and put it into a pan of boiling water.

Cover the pan and simmer slowly for 3 hours, adding more water if necessary to keep the haggis covered.

When cooked, remove from the pan and place on a warmed plate.

Remove the threads and slit open the bag.

Serve piping hot, with mashed potatoes, swedes and plenty of butter.

BOILED GIGOT OF MUTTON WITH CAPER SAUCE

Serves 8

The word 'gigot' for a leg of mutton or lamb is an inheritance from the days of the Auld Alliance with France.

1 leg of mutton
2 large onions, sliced
2 carrots
A sprig each of rosemary, parsley and thyme
1 bay leaf
6 black peppercorns
Salt

For the sauce:
2 oz (50 g) butter
2 oz (50 g) flour
1½ pints (900 ml/3¾ cups) stock from boiling the mutton
3 tablespoons capers and a little of the juice
Salt and pepper

Put the leg of mutton into a large saucepan and pour in enough cold water to come three-quarters of the way up.

Add the sliced onion, carrots, herbs and seasoning.

Cover and bring to the boil.

Simmer gently for 2 to 3 hours, or until the meat is tender.

Remove the meat from the saucepan and keep hot.

Skim the fat from the stock and strain off 1½ pints (900 ml/3¾ cups) for the sauce.

To make the sauce:

Melt the butter in another saucepan.

Stir in the flour, and cook gently for 1 minute.

Gradually add the stock, stirring all the time to prevent lumps. Add the capers and 1 tablespoon of the juice.

To serve:

Carve the leg of mutton and arrange on a warmed serving dish.

Cover with the caper sauce.

Serve with boiled potatoes and carrots.

MUTTON HAM

Meat used to be only an occasional luxury to the Highland crofter. When a sheep was killed the leg was often dry-salted to make a Mutton Ham. This is an old traditional method of curing.

1 gigot (leg) of mutton
8 oz (225 g) cooking salt
2 oz (50 g) bay salt
4 oz (100 g) moist brown sugar
½ oz (15 g) saltpetre
2 oz (50 g) black pepper
Half a dozen juniper berries

Place the mutton in a pickling pan.

Mix all the pickling ingredients together and pound well.

Heat half the mixture and rub it into the mutton.

Leave for 2 days.

Heat the other half of the mixture and rub it in.

Turn the mutton daily in the pickle for 2 weeks.

The leg of mutton should then be smoked — in the Highlands it would have been hung over a fire of peat with a juniper branch smouldering in the embers.

A smoked mutton ham keeps well for 2 to 4 months. When you want to eat it, soak in cold water for 2 hours before boiling in the same way as an ordinary ham, allowing 30 minutes per lb (450 g).

STUFFED ROAST GIGOT OF MUTTON

Serves 8

The French influence is evident in this recipe with the use of garlic.

A leg of mutton, boned
3 garlic cloves

For the stuffing:
2 oz (50 g) bacon
2 spring onions
A sprig of parsley
2 oz (50 g) shredded suet
4 oz (100 g) breadcrumbs
Salt and pepper

Ask your butcher to bone the leg of mutton.

Make slits with a sharp knife here and there over the skin.

Tuck a sliver of garlic into each.

Mince the bacon, spring onions and parsley.

Mix with the shredded suet and breadcrumbs.

Moisten with a little stock.

Press the stuffing into the cavity of the boned leg.

Sew up with a trussing needle and thread.

Roast in a moderate oven, allowing 20 minutes per lb (450 g).

Serve with roast potatoes and mashed turnip or swede, or boiled haricot beans.

Oven: 350°F/180°C   Gas Mark 4

PROSEN HOT POT

Serves 4

1½ lb (675 g) neck of mutton
2 onions
2 carrots
Salt and pepper
4 tomatoes
Stock

Ask your butcher to chop the mutton into smallish pieces.

Slice the onions and carrots.

Grease an ovenproof dish or casserole.

Arrange in it alternate layers of mutton, onion and carrot.

Season each layer with salt and pepper.

Skin the tomatoes and slice thinly.

Arrange the slices to cover the top of the hot pot.

Add enough stock to come halfway up the meat.

Cover and bake in a moderate oven for 2½ hours, or until the meat is tender.

Oven: 325°F/160°C   Gas Mark 3

ROAST SIRLOIN OF BEEF WITH HORSERADISH SAUCE

Sirloin may be cooked on the bone, or boned and rolled. Other joints suitable for roasting are wing rib (rib roast) and topside.

A joint of sirloin

For the sauce:
4 level tablespoons grated fresh horseradish
½ level teaspoon mustard powder
1 dessertspoon wine vinegar
1 level teaspoon caster sugar
A pinch of salt and pepper
¼ pint (150 ml/⅔ cup) double cream

Calculate the roasting time of the beef by allowing 20 minutes per lb (450 g) plus an extra 20 minutes. (If you want the beef rare, allow only 15 minutes per lb.)

Preheat the oven.

Put the joint into a roasting tin and roast for 20 minutes before reducing the temperature for the rest of the cooking time.

Leave the joint to stand for 10 minutes before carving.

To make the sauce:

Mix the horseradish, mustard, vinegar, sugar, salt and pepper together.

Whip the cream and stir in the other ingredients.

Serve the horseradish sauce in a small bowl to accompany the roast beef.

HIGHLAND BEEF BALLS   Serves 3-4

These beef balls should be highly flavoured, but the spices suggested
may be varied according to taste.

1 lb (450 g) minced beef
2 oz (50 g) suet
½ teaspoon ginger
½ teaspoon mace
½ teaspoon ground cloves
½ teaspoon dark brown sugar
Salt and pepper
1 egg, beaten
Medium oatmeal to coat
Oil for deep-frying

Mix the minced beef thoroughly with the suet, spices and
sugar.

Bind together with the beaten egg.

Divide the mixture into six or eight equal-sized pieces
and roll into balls.

Coat the balls in oatmeal.

Deep-fry for 5-7 minutes until the balls are a deep brown
colour.

SCOTCH BRAISED BEEF

Serves 4-6

1½ lb (675 g) topside of beef
4 oz (100 g) streaky bacon
1 carrot
1 stick of celery
1 small turnip
1 large onion
1 oz (25 g) butter
4 allspice berries
10 peppercorns
1 blade mace
1 sprig marjoram
1 sprig parsley
Salt and pepper
1½ pints (900 ml/3¾ cups) stock
1 oz (25 g) cornflour

Remove the rind from the bacon and cut into small pieces.

Dice the vegetables.

Melt the butter in a deep saucepan.

When smoking hot, add the bacon and vegetables and fry for 5 minutes, stirring frequently.

Remove the bacon and vegetables from the pan and fry the beef on all sides until it is browned and the juices are sealed in.

Put the bacon and vegetables back into the saucepan around the beef.

Tie the herbs into a muslin bag and add to the pan.

Season with salt and pepper.

Pour in the stock and bring to the boil.

Cover with the lid and simmer gently for 2-2½ hours, or until the meat is tender.

Lift the meat out on to a serving dish.

Remove the herb bag.

Mix the cornflour with a little cold water to a thin paste and stir into the stock.

Arrange the vegetables around the meat with a little of the gravy.

Serve the rest of the gravy in a sauceboat.

SCOTCH COLLOPS   Serves 4

1 lb (450 g) minced steak
1 oz (15 g) beef dripping
1 large onion
1 carrot
½ pint (300 ml/1¼ cups) stock
1 tablespoon oatmeal
Salt and pepper

Melt the dripping in a saucepan until it is smoking hot.

Put in the mince and allow to seal.

Cook until nicely browned all over.

Dice the onion and carrot and add to the meat.

Add the stock and oatmeal.

Season well with salt and pepper.

Allow to simmer slowly for about an hour until the mince is cooked and most of the liquid evaporated.

Serve with hot mashed potatoes and swedes.

BOILED BEEF WITH HODGILS   Serves 6

A joint of salt beef weighing 3-4 lbs (1.5-1.75 kg)
1 lb (450 g) onions
1 lb (450 g) carrots
1 small swede
1 bay leaf
1 tablespoon cornflour

For the hodgils:
8 oz (225 g) oatmeal
1 tablespoon chopped chives
Salt and pepper

Soak the beef overnight in cold water.

Calculate the cooking time at 25 minutes per lb (450 g).

Peel and slice the onions.

Cut the carrots and swede into cubes.

Put the beef into a large saucepan with the vegetables
and bay leaf.

Cover with cold water.

Bring to the boil and simmer for the calculated cooking
time.

To make the hodgils:

Mix the oatmeal with the chives and season well with salt
and pepper.

Skim some of the fat from the liquid in which the beef is
cooking and use to bind the oatmeal mixture together.

Divide the mixture into 8 or 10 equal-sized pieces and
roll into balls.

Add the hodgils to the meat and vegetables for the last 15
minutes of cooking time.

To serve:

Lift the meat out on to a serving dish and arrange the vegetables and hodgils around it.

Mix the cornflour to a thin paste with a little cold water.

Add to the liquid in which the beef was cooked to thicken it.

Serve the gravy separately in a sauceboat.

COLLOPS-IN-THE-PAN
Serves 4

4 thin slices of rump or fillet steak
2 oz (50 g) butter
4 onions
Salt and pepper
1 tablespoon walnut pickle or mushroom ketchup

Melt the butter in a large frying pan.

Slice the onions and cook gently in the butter until they are softened, but not browned.

Push the onions to the side and add the steaks.

Brown the steaks quickly on both sides.

Sprinkle with pepper.

Spread the onions around and amongst the steaks.

Cover the frying pan and cook gently for 10 minutes.

Lift the steaks out on to a warmed serving dish.

Add the walnut pickle or mushroom ketchup to the onion-gravy sauce in the pan.

Reheat and then pour over the steaks.

ABERDEEN SAUSAGE

Serves 8

This is an old farmhouse recipe for using up the end of a ham. If you use half pork instead of all beef this makes a more moist sausage. The sausage may be steamed or baked. Serve it cold with potato salad and baby beetroots.

1 lb (450 g) stewing beef
  (or 8 oz (225 g) beef and 8 oz (225 g) shoulder of pork)
12 oz (350 g) streaky bacon
1 onion
4 oz (100g) rolled oats
6 fresh sage leaves, finely chopped
A pinch of grated nutmeg
Salt and pepper
1 beaten egg
Browned breadcrumbs

Mince the beef (or beef and pork), bacon and onion.

Mix in the rolled oats, sage and nutmeg. Season well. Bind the mixture together with the beaten egg.

For the steaming method:

Mould the mixture into a sausage shape and wrap in greaseproof paper. Scald a pudding cloth and wrap the sausage in it, tying securely at the ends.

Bring a large pan of water to the boil and lower the sausage into it, preferably resting on a heatproof plate.

Cover, and simmer gently for 3 hours.

When cooked, remove the pudding cloth and greaseproof paper.

Roll in browned breadcrumbs while still hot.

For the baking method:

Press the sausage mixture into a greased ovenproof dish.

Cover with buttered greaseproof paper and then foil.

Stand the dish in a roasting tin and pour boiling water round it. Bake in a moderate oven for 2 hours.

When cooked, remove the foil and greaseproof paper and pour in a little hot stock.

Cover again with foil and put a weight on top to keep it firm. Leave overnight.

Next day, turn out the cooked sausage and coat well with browned breadcrumbs.

Oven: 350°F/180°C   Gas Mark 4

ABERDEEN MEAT ROLL

Serves 4

12 oz (375 g) lean steak mince
6 oz (175 g) streaky unsmoked bacon (minced)
1 beaten egg
4 tablespoons water
A little freshly ground black pepper
4 oz (100 g) fresh breadcrumbs
Extra breadcrumbs for coating

Mix together the steak mince, the minced bacon and breadcrumbs. Season with freshly ground black pepper.

Add the beaten egg and the water and stir to combine well.

Turn the mixture into a greased pudding basin, cover with greaseproof paper and tie down with string.

Put the pudding basin into a saucepan half filled with boiling water. Cover and steam for 2 hours.

Leave to cool slightly.

Turn the meat roll out and roll in the extra breadcrumbs.

Serve cold.

ROYAL GAME PIE

1 pheasant
Seasoned flour
6 oz (175 g) mushrooms
1 large onion
4 rashers of streaky bacon
1 tablespoon chopped parsley
A pinch of dried mixed herbs
¼ pint (150 ml/⅔ cup) stock
¼ pint (150 ml/⅔ cup) red wine or port
Salt and pepper
8 oz (225 g) puff pastry
Milk or beaten egg to glaze

Joint the pheasant.

Toss the pieces in the seasoned flour.

Arrange in a 2½ pint (1.5 litre) pie dish.

Slice the mushrooms, and peel and slice the onion.

Remove the rind from the bacon and chop into small pieces.

Add the mushrooms, onion and bacon to the pie dish.

Add the chopped parsley and herbs.

Pour over the stock and wine.

Season well with salt and pepper.

Roll out the pastry to make a lid to fit the pie dish, sealing it down with a little water.

Use any trimmings to make pastry leaves to decorate the pie.

Brush with milk or beaten egg to glaze.

Bake in a hot oven for 20 minutes, then reduce the heat and bake for a further 2 hours.

If necessary, cover the pie with greaseproof paper to stop the pastry from burning.

Oven: 425°F/220°C   Gas Mark 7
Reduce to: 325°F/160°C   Gas Mark 3

VEAL PIE

Serves 4

This dish dates back to the Auld Alliance with France. To make it really extravagant a chopped truffle can be added.

4 veal cutlets
½ teaspoon dried herbs
A pinch of ground mace
Salt and pepper
8 rashers of streaky bacon
2 boiled egg yolks or sweetbreads
8 oz (225 g) button mushrooms
Stock
8 oz (225 g) puff pastry

Lightly grease an ovenproof dish.

Season the veal with the herbs, mace, salt and pepper.

Place in the dish.

Remove the rind from the bacon rashers and roll each one up.

Tuck the rolls between the cutlets.

Add the egg yolks or sweetbreads, and the mushrooms.

Pour over enough stock to cover.

Roll out the pastry to make a lid.

Bake in a moderate oven for 1 hour.

Oven: 350°F/180°C   Gas Mark 4

MUTTON PIES

12 oz (350 g) lean mutton
A pinch of grated nutmeg
Salt and pepper
Stock

For the pastry:
1 lb (450 g) flour
A pinch of salt
4 oz (100 g) lard
½ pint (300 ml/1¼ cups) water

Chop the meat into small pieces, discarding any skin or gristle. Add the nutmeg. Season with salt and pepper.

Sift the flour and salt into a mixing basin.

Put the lard into a saucepan with the water and bring to the boil. Pour into the centre of the flour and mix well.

Leave until cool enough to handle, then knead until smooth.

Reserve a quarter of the pastry, keeping it warm and covered.

Divide the rest into 4 to 6 pieces. Roll out to line 4 to 6 small pie tins.

Fill the pastry cases with the meat mixture and moisten with stock.

Roll out 4 to 6 lids from the reserved pastry.

Press the edges together and make a hole in the top of each to allow steam to escape. Brush with beaten egg or milk to glaze.

Bake in a moderately hot oven for 40 minutes. When ready, fill up each pie through a funnel with more stock. Serve hot.

Oven: 375°F/190°C   Gas Mark 5

FORFAR BRIDIES

Serves 3 or 4

These are the Scottish equivalent of Cornish pasties, and are a speciality of Angus. Traditionally the pastry is made only of flour, salt and water, and no fat, but this makes it hard and tough on the outside. Rough puff or flaky pastry are good alternatives, though some Scottish cooks prefer to use shortcrust or suet pastry.

1 lb (450 g) topside or rump steak
3 oz (75 g) shredded suet
1 onion, minced
Salt and pepper
1 lb (450 g) rough puff or flaky pastry

Beat the meat well with a rolling pin and cut into thin strips about 1 inch (2.5 cm) long.

Mix with the suet and minced onion.

Season well with salt and pepper.

Divide the pastry into three or four equal pieces.

On a floured board roll each piece into a round or oval shape.

Cover half of each round with a third or quarter of the meat mixture.

Brush the edges with water.

Fold over the other half of the pastry, press and crimp the edges.

Make a small hole in the top of each to allow steam to escape.

Bake in a hot oven for 15 minutes, then reduce the temperature and bake for a further hour.

Serve hot, one per person.

Oven: 425°F/220°C   Gas Mark 7
Reduce to: 350°F/180°C   Gas Mark 4

MUSSELBURGH PIE

Serves 6-8

Oysters used to be plentiful along the coast near Edinburgh, and this sumptuous pie was made with oysters wrapped up inside the meat. These days mussels are a cheaper alternative.

3 lb (1.5 kg) mussels
1½ lbs (675 g) rump steak
1½ oz (40 g) beef suet
Seasoned flour
2 tablespoons oil
2 onions, finely chopped
½ pint (300 ml/1¼ cups) water
8 oz (225 g) puff pastry

Put the mussels in a pan of boiling salted water about 2 inches (5 cm) deep.

Cover with a lid and boil for 3 minutes.

Remove them from their shells.

Beat the steak until it is quite thin and cut into strips.

Place a few mussels and a piece of suet on each strip and roll up.

Dip each roll in seasoned flour and pack them into 2 pint (1 litre) pie dish round a pie funnel.

Heat the oil in a frying pan and cook the onions gently until golden brown.

Add the onions to the beef rolls in the pie dish.

Pour over the water.

Cover the dish with aluminium foil and cook in a moderate oven for 1½-2 hours, or until the meat is tender.

Remove from the oven and leave to cool.

Roll out the pastry to make a lid.

Use the trimmings to decorate the pie.

Brush with milk or beaten egg to glaze.

Make a few holes in the top for the steam to escape.

Bake in a hot oven for 30 minutes.

Oven: 350°F/180°C Gas Mark 4
Increase to: 425°F/220°C Gas Mark 7

STOVIES
Serves 4-6

This is a good way of using up left-over meat, poultry or game. The potatoes are stoved — that is, stewed in a pot on the cooker. Oatcakes and a glass of milk are the traditional accompaniments to this old Scots dish.

2 lbs (900 g) potatoes
1 large onion
2 oz (50 g) butter, lard, or meat dripping
Salt and pepper
½ pint (300 ml/1¼ cups) stock
8 oz (225 g) left-over meat, poultry or game
Chopped parsley for garnishing

Peel and slice the potatoes and onion.

Melt the fat in a large, heavy saucepan.

Fry the onion lightly, then add the potatoes.

Season well with salt and pepper.

Pour over the stock. Bring to the boil.

Cover with a tight-fitting lid.

Simmer gently for 1 hour, stirring occasionally to prevent sticking.

Add the left-over meat and cook for a further 10 minutes.

Garnish with the parsley and serve hot.

VENISON PATTIES

8 oz (225 g) cooked venison
Salt and pepper
A pinch of allspice
4 oz (100 g) prunes
¼ pint (150 ml/⅔ cup) red wine or port
½ pint (300 ml/1¼ cups) beef stock
8 oz (225 g) puff pastry

Mince the cooked venison and season well with salt, pepper and a pinch of allspice.

Stone the prunes and simmer in the port for 10 minutes.

Chop them finely and add to the meat.

Mix in the stock.

Roll out half the pastry to line flat patty tins.

Spoon in the meat mixture.

Dampen the edges with water and cover with lids made from the remaining pastry.

Seal and flute the edges.

Cut a small hole in the top of each.

Bake in a hot oven for 15-20 minutes, then reduce the temperature and bake for a further 40 minutes.

Eat hot or cold.

Oven: 425°F/220°C   Gas Mark 7
Reduce to: 375°F/190°C   Gas Mark 5

CLAPSHOT

Serves 6

A traditional dish from the Orkney Islands, clapshot is often served with haggis.

1 lb (450 g) potatoes
1 lb (450 g) turnips
A handful of chives
1 oz (25 g) butter or dripping
A little salt and freshly ground black pepper

Peel the potatoes and cut them into even-sized pieces.

Cut the thick rind off the turnips and cut into even-sized pieces.

Put the prepared vegetables into a large saucepan and bring to the boil.

Cover and simmer for about 20 minutes until the vegetables are soft.

Drain off the water and shake the vegetables over a low heat to dry them out slightly.

Mash them and stir in the butter or dripping until it has melted.

Season with a little salt and freshly ground black pepper.

Wash and snip the chives with a pair of kitchen scissors and stir them into the mixture.

Serve hot.

SCOTCH EGGS

5 hard-boiled eggs
Seasoned flour
1 lb (450 g) sausagemeat
1 beaten egg
Breadcrumbs
Oil for deep frying

Remove the shells from the hard-boiled eggs.

Dust the eggs with seasoned flour.

Divide the sausagemeat into 5 equal pieces.

On a floured surface flatten each piece into an oval shape large enough to cover an egg.

Place the egg in the centre and mould the sausagemeat round it, making sure the surface is free from cracks.

Coat each one in beaten egg.

Roll it in breadcrumbs, pressing the crumbs well in so that it is completely covered.

Heat the oil until it is really hot.

Carefully lower the Scotch eggs into the hot oil and cook for about 5-6 minutes, until brown all over.

Remove from the oil and drain well on kitchen paper.

Serve hot or cold.

POTTED HOUGH

Potting was a popular way of preserving meat, fish and game before the invention of refrigeration. This potted hough (shin of beef) is a tasty savoury dish for supper or high tea.

1 lb (450 g) hough (shin of beef)
A 2 lb (900 g) beef shin bone or knuckle of veal
1 level teaspoon salt
6 allspice berries
6 peppercorns
1 bay leaf

Put the meat and bone into a large pan and cover with cold water.

Bring to the boil and skim off any scum that rises to the surface.

Simmer for 3 to 4 hours until the meat is really tender.

Remove all meat from the bones and mince it.

Put into a wetted mould.

Return the bone to the sauce pan and add the salt, allspice berries, peppercorns and bayleaf.

Boil rapidly until the liquid has reduced by half.

Pour the stock over the meat in the mould.

Leave to set overnight.

When required, turn out the potted hough and serve with salad.

BASHED NEEPS

Neeps are large root vegetables known as swedes south of the border. In Scotland they are also referred to as turnips. This dish is traditionally served with haggis.

1 large swede or neep (about 2 lbs/1 kg)
A large pinch of salt
2 oz (50 g) dripping or butter
Freshly ground black pepper
A handful of chives

Remove the rind from the swede.

Cut the vegetable into small pieces and put these into a saucepan of boiling water.

Add a large pinch of salt and bring to the boil.

Simmer with the lid on for about 15 to 20 minutes or until the swede is very soft.

Drain the swede and add the dripping or butter.

Mash the swede well and season with the ground pepper.

Turn into a serving dish.

Snip the chives into tiny pieces with a pair of scissors and sprinkle on top of the mashed neeps.

Serve immediately.

CHAPPIT TATTIES

Serves 6

This potato dish is traditionally served with haggis.

1½ lbs (675 g) potatoes
2 oz (50 g) butter
4 tablespoons milk
A little salt and freshly ground black pepper

Peel the potatoes and cut into even-sized pieces.

Bring to the boil in a saucepan and simmer for about 20 minutes until soft.

Drain off the liquid and mash the potatoes.

Add the butter, milk, salt and pepper and beat well until the butter has melted and the potatoes are creamy.

Return the pan to the heat and cook gently stirring all the time to dry out the potatoes slightly.

Serve immediately.

PAN HAGGERTY

Serves 4

1 lb (450 g) potatoes
2 medium onions
2 oz (50 g) dripping
4 oz (100 g) cheese
A little salt and pepper

Peel and slice the potatoes and the onions.

Grate the cheese.

Melt the dripping in a large saucepan or deep frying pan.

Put in a layer of potatoes then onions then cheese and season with a little salt and pepper.

Repeat the layers until all the ingredients have been used.

Cover the pan and cook gently for about 45 minutes until the potatoes and onions are tender.

Remove the cover and place the pan under a hot grill to brown the cheese.

KAILKENNY   Serves 4-6

Kailkenny was eaten as a main meal rather than as an accompaniment. Left-over kailkenny may be made into flat rounds and fried.

1 lb (450 g) potatoes
1 lb (450 g) cabbage
8 oz (225 g) carrots
2 tablespoons double cream
A little salt and freshly ground blackpepper.

Peel and dice the potatoes.

Scrape and slice the carrots.

Wash and shred the cabbage.

Cook the vegetables in water until soft.

Mash the potatoes and carrots and mix with the cabbage.

Beat in the cream.

Season with a little salt and freshly ground black pepper.

Serve hot.

AYRSHIRE SWEET HAGGIS

Serves 6

Ayrshire is the area associated with the poet Robert Burns who was born in Alloway just south of Ayr. This dish is traditionally served on Saturday at high tea in the late afternoon. Any left over would be fried with rashers of Ayrshire bacon and served at breakfast the next day.

8 oz (225 g) medium oatmeal
4 oz (100 g) flour
8 oz (225 g) shredded suet
2 oz (50 g) soft brown sugar
2 oz (50 g) raisins
2 oz (50 g) currants
A little salt and pepper
Water

Put the oatmeal, flour, suet, sugar, raisins and currants into a bowl and mix well.

Season with a little salt and pepper.

Add enough water to bind the mixture together without making it wet.

Turn into a greased 2 pint (1.15 litre) pudding basin.

Cover with greaseproof paper and aluminium foil.

Put into a saucepan half full with boiling water.

Cover and steam for about 3 hours.

Serve hot.

Any left-overs may be sliced when cold and either fried or wrapped in aluminium foil and reheated in a moderate oven.

CROFTER'S PLUM PUDDING   Serves 4-6

This dish dates from around the end of the 19th century.

1 lb (450 g) flour
A pinch of salt
8 oz (225 g) shredded suet
8 oz (225 g) chopped raisins
1 large egg
About ½ pint (300 ml/1¼ cups) brown ale
½ teaspoon bicarbonate of soda

Sift the flour and salt into a large bowl.

Add the suet and raisins and mix well.

Beat the egg and add to the mixture.

Dissolve the bicarbonate of soda in a tablespoon of the ale and stir into the mixture.

Add enough of the remaining ale to make a stiff dropping consistency.

Turn the mixture into a greased 2 pint (1.15 litres) pudding basin.

Cover with a layer of greaseproof paper, then with a pudding cloth or piece of aluminium foil.

Place the basin in the upper part of a steamer or in a saucepan half full of boiling water.

Cover the steamer or saucepan with a tightly fitting lid and steam for about 3 hours.

Turn the pudding on to a hot dish and serve immediately.

CLOUTIE DUMPLING

Serves 6-8

This pudding is especially popular at Hogmanay and on birthdays. Coins wrapped in greaseproof paper are stirred into the mixture before it is cooked. Any left over can be fried for breakfast with bacon and eggs. Cloutie or clootie is the name of the cloth in which the pudding is traditionally cooked.

1 lb (450 g) self-raising flour
4 oz (100 g) shredded suet
4 oz (100 g) sugar
4 oz (100 g) currants
4 oz (100 g) raisins
1 teaspoon mixed spice
1 teaspoon cinnamon
1 large tablespoon treacle
Milk

Mix together the flour, suet, sugar, currants, raisins, mixed spice and the cinnamon.

Melt the treacle in a saucepan until runny.

Add the treacle to the dry ingredients.

Add enough milk to make a soft dough.

Put the mixture into a large damp cloth sprinkled generously with flour.

Tie the cloth around the dough loosely to allow the pudding to expand.

Put the pudding into a large saucepan of boiling water and steam for 2 hours.

Serve hot.

BORDER TART

The dough to make the base of this tart was originally a bread dough made with the weekly batch of bread. It can be made using a sweet shortcrust pastry base instead.

For the base:
6 oz (175 g) flour
3 oz (75 g) butter
1 oz (25 g) caster sugar
1 egg yolk

For the filling:
4 oz (100 g) marzipan
1 oz (25 g) flaked almonds
1 oz (25 g) chopped mixed peel
2 tablespoons raspberry jam

For the custard:
1 tablespoon cornflour
½ oz (15 g) butter
¼ pint (150 ml/⅔ cup) milk
1 egg yolk
1 oz (25 g) caster sugar
2 or 3 drops of vanilla essence

For the icing:
1 oz (25 g) icing sugar
A little warm water to mix

To make the base:

Sift the flour into a bowl and rub in the butter.

Stir in the sugar and add the beaten egg yolk.

Mix to make a firm dough and leave to rest for 30 minutes.

Roll out the dough to line an 8 inch (20 cm) flan ring.

Cut out 5 small circles about the size of 10 pence coins from any dough left over.

To make the custard:

Blend the cornflour into a tablespoon of the milk.

Stir in the remaining milk and the sugar.

Pour the liquid into a saucepan and slowly bring to the boil.

Simmer for a few minutes, stirring all the time.

Remove from the heat and stir in the butter until it has melted.

Beat in the egg yolk and the vanilla essence.

Leave to cool.

To make the tart:

Roll out the marzipan to fit the base of the tart.

Spread the marzipan with the jam and sprinkle the almonds and the mixed peel over this.

Spread the cooled custard over the filling.

Arrange the circles of dough on top of the custard.

Cover the tart with greaseproof paper or aluminium foil.

Bake for 20 minutes, reduce the oven temperature and bake for a further 20 minutes.

Mix the icing sugar with a little warm water to make a spreadable consistency and spread this over the circles of pastry.

Serve hot or cold.

Oven: 400°F/200°C   Gas Mark 6
Reduce to: 350°F/180°C   Gas Mark 4

APPLE FRUSHIE

Serves 6

This tart is popular in western Scotland.

For the pastry:
8 oz (225 g) flour
2 oz (50 g) butter
2 oz (50 g) lard
A pinch of salt
A little cold water to mix

For the filling:
12 oz (375 g) cooking apples
2 tablespoons clear runny heather honey
1 tablespoon rose-water

To make the pastry:

Sift the flour and salt together and rub in the butter and lard.

Add enough cold water to make a soft dough.

Leave to rest for 30 minutes.

Roll out ¾ of the dough to line a flan ring.

Roll out the remaining dough and cut out long strips.

To make the filling:

Peel, core and thinly slice the apples.

Arrange them in the pastry lined flan ring.

Sprinkle the rose-water and honey evenly over the apples.

Lay the strips of pastry over the filling to make a lattice pattern.

Bake for 30 minutes.

Sprinkle with caster sugar and serve with cream.

Oven: 375°F/190°C   Gas Mark 5

ECCLEFECHAN TARTS   Makes 12

Named after Ecclefechan, near Lockerbie in the south of Scotland, these small tarts are based on the popular Border Tart.

For the pastry:
4 oz (100 g) flour
2 oz (50 g) butter
1 oz (25 g) caster sugar
1 egg yolk

For the filling:
1 egg
2 oz (50 g) butter
3 oz (75 g) soft brown sugar
2 teaspoons white wine vinegar
4 oz (100 g) mixed dried fruit
2 oz (50 g) chopped walnuts

To make the pastry:

Sift the flour and rub in the butter until the mixture resembles breadcrumbs.

Stir in the sugar and the egg yolk to make a soft dough.

Leave the dough to rest for 30 minutes.

Roll out the dough thinly on a floured surface.

With a pastry cutter cut out 12 circles of dough and line 12 patty tins.

To make the filling:

Beat the egg and stir in the sugar and vinegar.

Melt the butter and beat into the egg mixture.

Add the dried fruit and the chopped walnuts.

Divide the filling between the pastry-lined patty tins.

Bake for 20 to 25 minutes. Serve hot or cold with cream.

Oven: 375°F/190°C   Gas Mark 5

BRYDON TART

This dish from the Highlands may be served warm as a dessert with cream, or cold as a tea-time cake.

8 oz (225 g) self-raising flour
3 oz (75 g) butter
3 oz (75 g) lard
4 oz (100 g) caster sugar
1 teaspoon ground cinnamon
2 eggs
4 tablespoons apricot jam
Icing sugar for sprinkling

Sift the flour and rub in the butter and lard.

Add the sugar and ground cinnamon.

Beat the eggs and stir into the mixture to make a stiff dough.

Divide the dough into two equal-sized pieces.

Roll out each piece into an 8 inch (20 cm) circle.

Place one circle in the bottom of a greased 8 inch (20 cm) flan ring with a loose bottom.

Spread the apricot jam over the circle to within ½ inch (1 cm) of the edge.

Cover with the remaining circle of dough and seal the edges.

Bake for 30 minutes.

Turn out the tart and sprinkle with icing sugar.

Oven: 400°F/200°C   Gas Mark 6

MARMALADE TART

Serves 6

For the pastry:
6 oz (175 g) flour
3 oz (75 g) butter
A little cold water to mix

For the filling:
3 eggs
4 tablespoons milk
4 tablespoons Dundee marmalade
2 oz (50 g) butter
2 oz (50 g) caster sugar

To make the pastry:

Sift the flour into a bowl and rub in the butter until the mixture resembles breadcrumbs.

Add enough cold water to make a soft dough.

Leave to rest for 30 minutes.

Roll out the pastry on a floured board and line an 8 inch (20 cm) flan ring.

To make the filling:

Melt the butter and pour into a bowl.

Add the eggs and beat well.

Add the milk, sugar and marmalade and beat until well combined.

Pour the filling into the pastry base.

Bake for 10 minutes in a hot oven then reduce the oven temperature and continue baking for a further 30 minutes or until the filling has set.

Oven: 400°F/200°C Gas Mark 6
Reduce to: 325°F/160°C   Gas Mark 3

CRANBERRY AND APPLE PIE

Serves 4-6

6 oz (175 g) puff pastry
1 egg
4 oz (100 g) caster sugar
1 oz (25 g) cornflour
A pinch of cinnamon
A pinch of allspice
A pinch of ground cloves
8 oz (225 g) cranberries
2 cooking apples
Juice of 1 orange

Butter a 2 pint (1.15 litres) pie dish.

Wash the cranberries.

Peel, core and slice the apples.

Put the cranberries and apple into the pie dish.

Mix the cornflour with the orange juice and stir until dissolved.

Add the sugar, cinnamon, allspice and ground cloves and mix well.

Pour the mixture over the cranberries and apple.

Roll out the pastry.

Moisten the edges of the pie dish and lay the pastry over the filling.

Brush the pastry with beaten egg for the glaze.

Bake at the higher oven temperature for 15 minutes then reduce the temperature and bake for a further 20 minutes.

Oven: 425°F/220°C   Gas Mark 7
Reduce to: 375°F/190°C   Gas Mark 5

MORAYSHIRE APPLES

Serves 6

The old county of Morayshire is now part of the Grampian region and is known as the 'Garden of the North'.

1½ lbs (675 g) cooking apples
¼ pint (150 ml/⅔ cup) water
4 oz (100 g) caster sugar
A pinch of ground cloves
3 oz (75 g) shredded suet
6 oz (175 g) medium oatmeal
2 oz (50 g) ground hazelnuts
4 oz (100 g) soft brown sugar

Put the caster sugar and the pinch of ground cloves into a small saucepan with the water.

Heat gently and stir until the sugar has dissolved.

Peel, core and slice the apples into a large pie dish.

Pour the sugared water over the apples.

Mix together the suet, oatmeal, hazelnuts and half of the soft brown sugar.

Sprinkle this mixture over the apples.

Sprinkle the remaining soft brown sugar over the top.

Bake for 45 to 50 minutes or until the top is browned.

Serve hot with cream.

Oven: 350°F/180°C   Gas Mark 4

DRUMLANRIG PUDDING

Serves 6-8

This pudding is named after Drumlanrig Castle which was built around 1680 just north of Dumfries.

2 lbs (1 kg) rhubarb
6 oz (175 g) caster sugar
6 large slices of white bread
1 tablespoon water

Chop the rhubarb and put into a saucepan with the water and sugar.

Bring to the boil, cover and simmer very gently for about 15 minutes or until the rhubarb is soft.

Grease a 2 pint (1.15 litres) pudding basin or pie dish.

Put a layer of bread in the base.

Pour some rhubarb over the bread.

Add another layer of bread followed by some more rhubarb and continue adding layers until the dish is full, finishing with a layer of bread.

Cover with a piece of greaseproof paper and put a weight on top.

Leave the pudding in a cool place for at least 24 hours.

Loosen the pudding around the edges and turn out on to a serving plate.

Serve with cream.

TIPSY LAIRD

Serves 6

6 trifle sponges
3 tablespoons raspberry jam
3 oz (75 g) ratafia biscuits or macaroons
Grated rind of ½ lemon
¼ pint (150 ml/⅔ cup) sherry
1 pint (600 ml/2½ cups) cold custard
¼ pint (150 ml/⅔ cup) double cream
1 tablespoon Drambuie
Blanched flaked almonds to decorate

Split the trifle sponges in half lengthways.

Spread the halves with jam then sandwich them together and place them in a shallow dish.

Crumble the ratafia biscuits or macaroons and scatter them over the sponge.

Sprinkle the grated lemon rind on top.

Pour the sherry over the sponge and biscuits and leave for 1 hour.

Whisk the cold custard until creamy and spoon over the contents of the dish.

Whisk the cream and the Drambuie together until the mixture holds its shape.

Spread the flavoured cream over the custard.

Decorate with flaked almonds.

Serve chilled.

APPLE CHARLOTTE

Serves 4

6 oz (175 g) self-raising flour
2 oz (50 g) caster sugar
4 oz (100 g) butter
1 egg
1½ lbs (675 g) cooking apples
Icing sugar

Peel, core and slice the apples into a saucepan and add a very little water.

Stew the apples until soft.

Cream the butter and sugar until light and fluffy.

Gradually beat in the egg with a little of the flour.

Stir in the remaining flour to make a soft dough.

Roll out ½ of the dough to line a greased 7 inch (18 cm) sandwich tin.

Pour the apples on top and spread them to the edges of the dough.

Roll out the remaining dough and lay over the filling, moistening the edges to seal well.

Bake for 1 hour.

Turn out and dredge with icing sugar.

Oven: 325°F/160°C Gas Mark 3.

CRANNACHAN

This dessert is traditionally served at harvest celebrations and at Hallowe'en. It is made using the traditional soft cheese called crowdie made in the Highlands.

2 oz (50 g) lightly toasted medium oatmeal
4 tablespoons malt whisky
3 tablespoons clear heather honey
4 oz (100 g) crowdie or cream cheese
8 oz (225 g) raspberries
¼ pint (150 ml/⅔ cup) double cream

Mix the oatmeal, whisky and 1 tablespoon of the honey in a bowl and leave for about 12 hours.

Stir in the cream cheese or crowdie and then the raspberries.

Whisk the cream until it holds its shape.

Put half of the cream into a dish or into individual glasses.

Spoon the oatmeal and cream cheese mixture over.

Cover with the remaining cream.

Pour the rest of the honey over the top.

Serve chilled.

FORTUNE TELLING CROWDIE
Serves 4

> 'A coin for wealth
> A ring for marriage
> A button for a bachelor
> A thimble for a spinster
> A wishbone for your heart's desire.'

Small silver charms were stirred into this dessert. Each charm had a special meaning. The dessert was eaten on the night of Hallowe'en and each guest would hope to find a favourable charm in his or her portion.

2 oz (50 g) lightly toasted medium oatmeal
½ pint (300 ml/1¼ cups) double cream
1 oz (25 g) caster sugar
1 tablespoon dark rum

Whip the cream until it holds its shape.

Stir in the sugar and rum and whisk again until thick.

Gently stir in the toasted oatmeal. Chill well.

CALEDONIAN CREAM
Serves 4-6

2 tablespoons Dundee Marmalade
2 tablespoons brandy or whisky
Juice of ½ lemon
½ pint (300 ml/1¼) double cream
1 oz (25 g) caster sugar

Put the marmalade, sugar and the lemon juice into a saucepan and heat gently until the sugar has dissolved.

Remove from the heat and allow to cool.

Transfer the mixture to a bowl and add the cream and the brandy or whisky.

Whisk the mixture until thick.

Spoon the cream into individual glasses and chill.

LOTHIAN GINGERBREAD

8 oz (225 g) flour
1 teaspoon bicarbonate of soda
2 teaspoons ground ginger
1 teaspoon ground cinnamon
A pinch of salt
6 oz (175 g) butter
6 oz (175 g) treacle
4 oz (100 g) soft brown sugar
6 tablespoons milk
2 eggs
2 oz (50 g) sultanas
2 oz (50 g) chopped walnuts

Place the butter, treacle and sugar into a saucepan and heat gently until well combined.

Remove from the heat and stir in the milk and eggs.

Sift the flour, salt, ginger, cinnamon and bicarbonate of soda together.

Make a well in the centre and gradually beat in the treacle mixture until the batter is smooth.

Stir in the sultanas and chopped walnuts.

Pour into a greased and lined 2 lb (1 kg) loaf tin.

Bake for 1¼ hours.

Oven: 325°F/160°F   Gas Mark 3

SCOTTISH BLACK BUN

'Bun' is an old Scottish word for a fruity cake which is eaten at Hogmanay. It was originally baked enclosed in bread dough to retain the moisture and flavour, but is now more commonly encased in a pastry dough. The case was discarded before the cake was eaten. As with all good fruit cakes it is at its best at least 2 weeks after it is made. It should be kept wrapped in greaseproof paper and aluminium foil in an airtight tin.

For the pastry case:
8 oz (225 g) flour
1 teaspoon bicarbonate of soda
A pinch of salt
2 oz (50 g) butter
2 oz (50 g) lard

For the cake:
8 oz (225 g) flour
3 teaspoons allspice
1 teaspoon bicarbonate of soda
1 teaspoon cream of tartar
4 oz (100 g) brown sugar
12 oz (375 g) currants
12 oz (375 g) raisins
4 oz (100 g) ground almonds
2 oz (50 g) chopped mixed candied peel
2 tablespoons brandy
¼ pint (150 ml/⅔ cup) milk
1 beaten egg

To make the pastry case:

Sift the flour, salt and bicarbonate of soda into a bowl.

Rub in the butter and lard until the mixture resembles breadcrumbs.

Add enough cold water to make a soft dough.

Leave the dough to rest for 30 minutes.

Roll out ⅔ of the dough to line a greased and lined 8 inch (20 cm) cake tin.

To make the cake:

Sift together the flour, allspice, bicarbonate of soda and the cream of tartar.

Add the sugar, currants, raisins, ground almonds and the chopped mixed candied peel.

Pour in the brandy and the milk and mix well.

Turn the mixture into the prepared pastry dough case.

Turn over the top edge of the dough and moisten the edges with water.

Roll out the remaining pastry dough and place over the cake mixture pressing the edges of the dough together securely.

Brush with beaten egg.

Plunge a skewer right through the pastry case and the cake four times.

Cover the top with greaseproof paper.

Bake for 30 minutes then lower the oven temperature and bake for a further 2 hours.

Oven: 400°F/200°C   Gas Mark 6
Reduce to: 325°F/160°C   Gas Mark 3

DUNDEE CAKE

Popular in the 19th century in Dundee this cake became famous throughout the country. It should be covered with whole almonds.

10 oz (275 g) self-raising flour
A teaspoon mixed spice
A pinch of salt
8 oz (225 g) butter
8 oz (225 g) caster sugar
5 eggs
Grated rind of 1 lemon
2 oz (50 g) ground almonds
6 oz (175 g) raisins
6 oz (175 g) currants
6 oz (175 g) sultanas
2 oz (50 g) chopped mixed peel
3 oz (75 g) blanched whole almonds
1 tablespoon brandy
A little milk to mix

Cream the butter and sugar together until light and fluffy.

Gradually beat in the eggs one at a time with a little of the flour to prevent the mixture from curdling.

Sift in the remaining flour, salt, ground almonds and the mixed spice stirring gently.

Stir in the grated lemon rind, the raisins, currants, sultanas and the mixed peel.

Stir in the brandy and enough of the milk to make a fairly soft dropping consistency.

Turn into a greased and lined 8 inch (20 cm) cake tin.

Smooth the top with a palette knife and arrange the almonds to cover the surface of the mixture.

Place a circle of greaseproof paper on top of the cake and leave it to rest for a couple of hours. This helps to prevent the dried fruit from sinking.

Bake in the centre of the oven for 3 hours.

Remove from the oven but leave the cake in the tin for at least 20 minutes before turning out, then cool on a wire rack.

Keep for at least 2 weeks in an airtight tin before using.

Oven: 325°F/160°C   Gas Mark 3

ANGUS FRUITCAKE

1 lb (450 g) flour
1 lb (450 g) cooking apples
2 tablespoons golden syrup or honey
6 oz (175 g) butter
2 teaspoons mixed spice
2 teaspoons bicarbonate of soda
1 egg
½ pint (300 ml/1¼ cups) buttermilk

Put the golden syrup or honey into a saucepan.

Peel, core and slice the apples and add to the syrup or honey.

Cover and simmer for about 10 to 15 minutes until the apples are soft. Leave to cool.

Sift the flour, mixed spice and bicarbonate of soda into a bowl. Rub in the butter.

Beat the egg and buttermilk together and gradually add to the flour. Stir in the apples and syrup.

Mix well to make a soft dropping consistency.

Turn into a greased and lined 7 inch (18 cm) cake tin.

Bake for 1½ hours.

Oven: 350°F/180°C   Gas Mark 4

SELKIRK BANNOCK

This rich fruit bread is said to have been enjoyed by Queen Victoria. It was first made in Selkirk in south-eastern Scotland around the mid-19th century.

1 lb (450 g) strong plain flour
1 oz (25 g) fresh yeast
4 oz (100 g) caster sugar
7 fl oz (200 ml/¾ cup) warm milk
1 teaspoon salt
2 oz (50 g) lard
2 oz (50 g) butter
8 oz (225 g) sultanas
1 beaten egg
A little extra caster sugar for glazing

Crumble the yeast into the warm milk and add a teaspoon of the sugar. Stir until the sugar has dissolved and leave for 15 minutes or until frothy.

Sift the flour into a bowl and add the salt.

Rub in the butter and lard.

Add the remaining sugar.

Gradually add the yeast liquid to the mixture to make a fairly soft dough.

Knead on a floured surface for 10 minutes until smooth and elastic.

Put the dough into a bowl, cover with a damp cloth and leave in a warm place until doubled in size.

Knock back the dough and knead in the sultanas and the sugar.

Shape into 2 small rounds or 1 large round and place on a greased baking sheet.

Leave in a warm place for about 30 minutes to prove.

Bake for 30 minutes then remove the bannocks from the oven.

Glaze the top with beaten egg and sprinkle with a little caster sugar.

Return to the oven for a further 20 to 30 minutes.

Cool on a wire rack.

Serve, thinly sliced, and spread with butter.

Oven: 350°F/180°C   Gas Mark 4

ORKNEY BROONIE

This delicious cake is rather like a rich gingerbread. It should be made at least a week before it is needed since it is better when left to mature.

8 oz (225 g) fine oatmeal
4 oz (100 g) self-raising flour
4 oz (100 g) butter
A pinch of salt
4 oz (100 g) soft brown sugar
2 teaspoons ground ginger
1 teaspoon bicarbonate of soda
2 oz (50 g) treacle
4 oz (100 g) golden syrup
1 egg
¼ pint (150 ml/⅔ cup) buttermilk

Mix the oatmeal and flour in a bowl and rub in the butter.

Add the salt, sugar, ginger and bicarbonate of soda.

Stir in the treacle and golden syrup.

Beat the egg and buttermilk together and add to the mixture.

Grease and line an 8 inch (20 cm) square tin and pour the mixture into the tin.

Bake for 30 to 40 minutes.

Oven: 350°F/180°C   Gas Mark 4

SCOTTISH SHORTBREAD

This shortbread was originally made with fine oatmeal but it is now common to use both wheat flour and rice flour. It is found in a variety of shapes and thicknesses according to the part of Scotland in which it is made. It is traditionally eaten at Christmas and at Hogmanay.

4 oz (100 g) flour
2 oz (50 g) rice flour or ground rice
4 oz (100 g) caster sugar
4 oz (100 g) butter
Extra caster sugar for sprinkling

Sift the flour and rice flour or ground rice together.

Add the sugar and rub in the butter.

Lightly knead the dough on a floured board until smooth.

Press the dough into a floured mould or into a greased and lined baking tin.

Prick the dough with a fork and bake for about 25 minutes or until it is beginning to turn brown.

Remove from the oven and cut the shortbread into fingers but leave it in the tin or mould to cool.

Sprinkle with caster sugar to serve.

Oven: 375°F/190°C   Gas Mark 5

PETTICOAT TAILS

This thin, crisp and shaped shortbread is a speciality of Edinburgh. There is some controversy over the origin of its name. Some sources say that it takes its shape and is named after the bell-hoop petticoats worn by fashionable ladies in the 19th century. Others say the name is more likely to be a corruption of the French name for little cakes — 'petites gatelles'.

8 oz (225 g) flour
2 oz (50 g) rice flour
4 oz (100 g) butter
1 oz (25 g) lard
A little milk to mix
2 oz (50 g) caster sugar
1 teaspoon caraway seeds
Caster sugar for sprinkling

Sift the flour and the rice flour together.

Add the sugar and caraway seeds.

Rub in the butter and lard.

Add enough milk to make a firm dough.

Knead gently on a floured surface.

Roll out to a thickness of about ¼ inch (5 mm).

Cut out a large circle the size of a dinner plate.

Cut out a small circle about 4 inches (10 cm) in diameter in the middle.

Crimp the outer edges with a finger and thumb.

Cut the outer ring into 8 segments or petticoat tails.

Prick each segment 2 or 3 times with a fork and place them on a greased baking sheet.

Bake for 20 to 25 minutes or until golden brown.

Remove from the oven and sprinkle with caster sugar.

Leave the petticoat tails to cool then reassemble the pattern on a large plate or tray.

Oven: 350°F/180°C   Gas Mark 4

AYRSHIRE SHORTBREAD

Unlike other shortbreads, this shortbread is made with cream.

6 oz (175 g) flour
2 oz (50 g) rice flour or ground rice
4 oz (100 g) butter
3 oz (75 g) caster sugar
1 egg yolk
2 tablespoons cream

Sift the flour into a bowl and add the rice flour or ground rice and sugar.

Rub in the butter.

Beat the egg yolk and the cream together and add to the mixture.

Work the mixture into a dough and knead this lightly on a floured surface until smooth.

Roll out the dough to a thickness of about ¼ inch (5 mm).

Cut out circles with a small pastry cutter.

Place the circles on a greased baking sheet.

Bake for 15 minutes.

Oven: 350°F/180°C   Gas Mark 4

SCONES

Scones probably originated from the Dutch 'Schoonhrot', a kind of square cake made in the 16th century. They were traditionally cooked on an iron girdle which was rubbed with salt and not greased. To make the best scones, handle as little as possible and make as quickly as possible.

GIRDLE SCONES   Makes 4

8 oz (225 g) flour
1 teaspoon bicarbonate of soda
½ teaspoon cream of tartar
A pinch of salt
½ oz (15 g) caster sugar
¼ pint (150 ml/⅔ cup) buttermilk

Pre-heat the girdle or a lightly greased frying pan.

Sift the flour, bicarbonate of soda, cream of tartar and salt into a bowl.

Add the sugar and mix well.

Add enough buttermilk to make a fairly stiff dough.

Knead lightly on a floured board until smooth.

Roll out the dough to make a circle about ½ inch (1 cm) thick.

Cut the circle into quarters.

Cook the quarters on a hot girdle for about 10 minutes on each side or until risen and beginning to brown.

Wrap in a clean cloth and cool on a rack.

SOUR SCONES

8 oz (225 g) fine oatmeal
½ pint (300 ml/1¼ cups) buttermilk
8 oz (225 g) flour
1 teaspoon bicarbonate of soda
A pinch of salt
1 teaspoon caraway seeds
1 oz (25 g) caster sugar

Soak the oatmeal in the buttermilk overnight.

Sift the flour, bicarbonate of soda and salt into a bowl.

Stir in the caraway seeds and sugar.

Add the oatmeal and buttermilk and mix to a soft dough.

Divide the dough into two equal sized pieces.

Roll out each piece of dough on a floured board to make a circle about ½ inch (1 cm) thick.

Cut each circle into 8 triangles and bake on a hot girdle for 5 to 10 minutes on each side.

Wrap the scones in a cloth and cool on a wire rack.

BARLEY SCONES

8 oz (225 g) barley flour
½ teaspoon bicarbonate of soda
½ teaspoon cream of tartar
½ oz (15 g) butter
A pinch of salt
About ¼ pint (150 ml/⅔ cup) buttermilk

Mix the flour, bicarbonate of soda, cream of tartar and salt together.

Rub in the butter.

Add enough of the buttermilk to make a soft dough.

Knead the dough lightly on a floured board.

Roll out to make a large circle about ½ inch (1 cm) thick.

Cut the circle into 8 triangles.

Bake the scones on a hot girdle for about 5 to 10 minutes on each side.

Wrap in a clean cloth and cool on a rack.

POTATO SCONES

Makes 8

12 oz (375 g) potatoes
5 oz (150 g) flour
1 egg
½ oz (15 g) butter
A pinch of salt

Peel and boil the potatoes until soft.

Add a pinch of salt and mash them with the butter and the egg.

Sift in half of the flour and mix well.

Add enough of the remaining flour to make a soft but not a sticky dough.

Knead lightly on a floured surface until smooth.

Divide the mixture into two equal pieces.

Roll out each half to make a circle about ½ inch (1 cm) thick.

Cut each circle into quarters.

Cook the scones on a hot girdle or a lightly greased frying pan for about 5 minutes on each side.

Wrap them in a clean cloth and cool on a rack.

Serve with butter or honey.

BRIDE'S BONN

This is a recipe from the Shetland Islands and is also known as Bride's Bun and Bridal Cake. The cake was traditionally made on the wedding day by the bride's mother who then held it over her daughter's head and broke it as the bride entered her new home as a married woman. The bride and bridegroom had to eat all the pieces of the cake to ensure a happy marriage.

5 oz (150 g) self-raising flour
1 teaspoon baking powder
2 oz (50 g) butter
1 oz (25 g) caster sugar
½ teaspoon caraway seeds
A little milk to mix

Sift the flour and the baking powder into a bowl and rub in the butter.

Stir in the sugar and caraway seeds.

Add enough milk to make a stiff dough.

Knead the dough lightly on a floured board and roll out into a round about ½ inch (1 cm) thick.

Cut the round into quarters.

Bake on a hot girdle for 5 to 10 minutes in each side.

These are best served the same day.

FATTY CUTTIES

This recipe comes from the Orkney Islands.

6 oz (175 g) flour
½ teaspoon bicarbonate of soda
2 oz (50 g) caster sugar
3 oz (75 g) currants
3 oz (75 g) butter

Pre-heat the girdle or a heavy frying pan.

Sift the flour and the soda into a bowl.

Add the sugar and currants and stir well.

Melt the butter in a pan and stir into the mixture to make a stiff dough.

Knead gently on a floured board until smooth.

Divide the dough into two equally sized pieces and roll each piece into a circle about ¼ inch (5 mm) thick.

Cut each circle into 4 or 6 triangles.

Cook the triangles on a hot girdle for about 5 minutes on each side.

Wrap in a cloth and cook on a rack.

Serve the same day.

OATCAKES

True oatcakes are made using no flour. They were originally baked on a hot girdle. They can be fairly tricky to make. The secret is to make only enough dough for one baking and to roll out the mixture while the water is still hot.

4 oz (100 g) medium oatmeal
A pinch of salt
½ teaspoon bicarbonate of soda
½ oz (15 g) dripping or lard
3 tablespoons hot water
Extra medium oatmeal for rolling

Mix the salt and bicarbonate of soda with the oatmeal.

Rub in the fat.

Add 3 tablespoons of very hot water.

Mix quickly to make a slightly sticky dough.

Roll out the dough very thinly on a surface lightly sprinkled with oatmeal.

Cut out circles with a pastry cutter.

Put the oatcakes on to a greased baking sheet and rub them with oatmeal.

Bake for 20 minutes.

Turn each oatcake over with a palette knife and bake for a further 10 minutes.

Cool on a wire rack and store in an airtight tin.

Serve warm either by toasting lightly or heating in a low oven.

Oven: 350°F/180°C   Gas Mark 4

FIFE BANNOCKS

Bannocks are baked on a girdle and are thicker and heavier than oatcakes. They are made all over Scotland and the choice of ingredients reflect the type of grain grown locally. In Fife, wheat is the staple grain.

6 oz (175 g) flour
½ oz (15 g) butter
4 oz (100 g) fine oatmeal
1 teaspoon bicarbonate of soda
1 teaspoon cream of tartar
½ oz (15 g) caster sugar
A pinch of salt
¼ pint (150 ml/⅔ cup) buttermilk

Sift the flour, salt, bicarbonate of soda and cream of tartar into a bowl.

Rub in the butter.

Stir in the oatmeal and sugar.

Add enough buttermilk to make a stiff dough.

Knead lightly on a floured surface until smooth.

Roll out into a round about ½ inch (1 cm) thick.

Divide the round into 8 and cook on a hot girdle for about 5 to 10 minutes on each side.

Serve warm.

DROPPED SCONES

Makes about 16

'Scone' is derived from the Gaelic word 'sgonn' and is pronounced 'skon'.

4 oz (100 g) flour
1 teaspoon bicarbonate of soda
1 teaspoon cream of tartar
A pinch of salt
1 oz (25 g) caster sugar
1 egg
¼ pint (150 ml/⅔ cup) milk

Sift the flour, bicarbonate of soda, cream of tartar and salt into a bowl.

Stir in the sugar.

Beat the egg and milk together and gradually add to the dry ingredients stirring all the time to prevent any lumps forming.

Put tablespoonsful of the batter on to a hot girdle or lightly greased frying pan.

Cook until bubbles appear on the surface of each pancake and the underside is golden brown.

Turn each pancake over with a palette knife and cook the other side until golden.

Serve warm with butter.

SCOTTISH BAPS

Makes 8-10

1 oz (25 g) fresh yeast
1 teaspoon caster sugar
¼ pint (150 ml/⅔ cup) warm water
¼ pint (150 ml/⅔ cup) milk
1 lb (450 g) strong plain flour
2 teaspoons salt
2 oz (50 g) butter

Dissolve the sugar in the water which should be hand hot.

Crumble in the yeast, stir then leave for about 15 minutes or until frothy.

Sift the flour and salt into a bowl.

Rub in the butter.

Gradually add the yeast mixture.

Add enough of the milk to make a soft dough that is not too sticky.

Turn the dough out on to a floured board and knead for about 10 minutes until it is smooth and elastic.

Put the dough into a bowl and cover with a clean damp cloth.

Leave in a warm place until the dough has doubled in size.

Knock back and knead again.

Divide the mixture into 8 or 10 pieces and shape each piece into a flattish round.

Place the baps on greased baking sheets, cover with a clean cloth and leave to rise in a warm place.

Sprinkle the baps with a little flour and bake for 15 to 20 minutes.

Oven: 400°F/200°C   Gas Mark 6

BUTTERY ROWIES

Makes 16

Similar to French croissants, rowies are also known as Aberdeen But-
teries and are commonly served warm for breakfast in Aberdeen and
north-eastern Scotland.

1 lb (450 g) strong white flour
1 oz (25 g) fresh yeast
1 teaspoon caster sugar
½ pint (300 ml/1¼ cups) lukewarm water and milk
   mixed
1 teaspoon salt
6 oz (175 g) butter
6 oz (175 g) lard
1 egg yolk to glaze

Stir the sugar into half of the lukewarm milk and water
mixture and crumble in the yeast.

Stir and leave for 10 to 15 minutes until frothy.

Sift the flour and salt into a bowl.

Gradually add the yeast mixture and extra liquid to
make a firm dough.

Knead for about 10 minutes on a floured board until the
dough is smooth and elastic.

Put the dough into a bowl and cover with a clean damp
cloth.

Leave in a warm place until doubled in size.

Knock back the dough and knead for a few minutes.

Roll out into a large rectangle about ½ inch (1 cm) thick.

Spread one third of the butter and one third of the lard
on to the top two-thirds of the dough.

Fold up the bottom third of the dough and fold down
the top third.

Seal the edges, turn it round and roll the dough out
again.

Leave in a cool place for 10 minutes.

Spread another third of the fats on to the dough and continue as before leaving it to rest for 10 minutes before spreading the remaining fat over.

Finally roll out the dough to a thickness of about ½ inch (1 cm) and divide it into 16 squares.

Shape these pieces into ovals and place them on greased and floured baking sheets.

Put them into a warm place to prove for about 30 minutes.

Brush each buttery with beaten egg yolk and bake for 15 to 20 minutes until nicely browned.

Serve warm with buter.

Oven: 425°F/220°C   Gas Mark 7

OATMEAL THISTLE BUNS   Makes about 20

For the pastry:
6 oz (175 g) flour
3 oz (75 g) butter
A pinch of salt
A little cold water to mix

For the bread dough:
1 lb (450 g) strong plain flour
1 oz (25 g) fresh yeast
1 tablespoon runny heather honey
18 fl oz (550 ml/2 cups) hand-hot water
2 teaspoons salt
10 oz (275 g) fine oatmeal
2 egg yolks

To make the pastry:

Sift the flour and salt together and rub in the butter.

Add enough cold water to make a soft dough.

Leave the dough to rest for 30 minutes.

Roll out the dough on a lightly floured board and cut out 20 thistle shapes.

To make the bread dough:

Stir the honey into the hand-hot water and crumble in the yeast.

Leave the mixture for 15 minutes until frothy.

Meanwhile mix the flour, salt and 8 oz (225 g) of the oatmeal in a bowl.

Gradually pour in the yeast liquid to make a firm dough.

Sprinkle the remaining oatmeal on to a clean surface and knead the dough on this for about 10 minutes until smooth and elastic.

Place the dough in a bowl and cover with a damp cloth.

Leave in a warm place until the dough has doubled in size.

Knock back the dough and knead for 5 minutes then divide the dough into 20 pieces and make each piece into a ball.

Place the balls of dough on two lightly greased baking sheets and leave in a warm place for about 30 minutes or until doubled in size.

Brush each ball of bread dough with a little egg yolk and place a pastry dough thistle on top of each one.

Brush with egg yolk to glaze and bake for 20 minutes or until golden brown and well risen.

Serve warm with butter.

Oven: 425°F/220°C   Gas Mark 7

OATMEAL PASTRY

This is an excellent pastry for fruit tarts. It makes enough to line an 8 inch (20 cm) flan ring.

3 oz (75 g) self-raising flour
3 oz (75 g) fine oatmeal
2 oz (50 g) butter
1 oz (25 g) lard
½ oz (15 g) caster sugar
A little cold water to mix

Sift the flour into a bowl and stir in the oatmeal.

Rub in the lard and butter until the mixture resembles breadcrumbs.

Stir in the sugar.

Add enough cold water to make a fairly stiff dough.

Leave to rest for 30 minutes.

Roll out the dough on a floured board.

Use to line an 8 inch (20 cm) flan ring.

Bake blind in a hot oven for 10 minutes to set the pastry before adding the filling.

Oven: 400°F/200°C   G Mark 6

PORRIDGE

Serves 2

Porridge is one of the best-known Scottish specialities. Usually eaten for breakfast, it is filling and makes a good start to the day especially when about to spend a long day in the hills. It is said that porridge should be eaten standing up.

1 pint (600 ml/2½ cups) water
2½ oz (65 g) medium oatmeal
A pinch of salt

Put the water into a saucepan and bring to the boil.

Add the oatmeal while stirring to prevent any lumps forming.

Cover and simmer gently for about 15 minutes.

Add the salt and stir it in well.

Cover the pan again and simmer for a further 10 minutes or until the porridge is fairly thick.

Porridge is traditionally served hot with separate bowls of cream or milk. Each spoonful of porridge is dipped into the cream or milk and then eaten.

BREAD SAUCE

Bread sauce was first made in Scotland and is served with poultry and game birds.

3 oz (75 g) white breadcrumbs
1 onion
3 cloves
3 peppercorns
A blade of mace
½ pint (300 ml/1¼ cups) milk
½ oz (15 g) butter
1 tablespoon cream
A little salt and pepper

Put the milk into a saucepan with the blade of mace, the cloves and the peppercorns.

Chop the onion and add to the milk.

Bring to the boil, remove from the heat, cover and leave for 1 hour.

Strain the milk.

Add the breadcrumbs and return to the heat.

Bring to the boil and simmer until the sauce thickens.

Season with a little salt and pepper.

Beat in the butter and cream.

Serve hot.

ROWAN AND CRAB APPLE JELLY

Makes about 4 lbs (1.75 kg)

Rowan trees were planted gardens particularly in the west coast of Scotland as they were thought to ward off evil Spirits. It is best to pick the rowan berries in the autumn just before they change from orange to dark red in colour.

2 lbs (1 kg) rowan berries
2 lbs (1 kg) crab apples
About 1 lb (450 g) granulated sugar
Peel of ½ lemon
1 clove

Wash the rowan berries and remove any stalks.

Wash and halve the crab applies.

Put the fruit into a large saucepan and add enough water to cover.

Bring to the boil and simmer until the fruit is soft and pulpy.

Strain through a jelly bag or muslin until the dripping has stopped. Do not squeeze the bag or the jelly will be cloudy.

Measure the juice and add 1 lb (450 g) sugar to every pint (600 ml/2½ cups) of the juice.

Return the juice to the pan and stir over a low heat until the sugar has dissolved.

Put the lemon peel and clove into a muslim bag and add to the pan.

Bring to the boil and boil rapidly until the mixture reaches setting point. If a little of the jelly sets when it is put on a cold saucer setting point has been reached.

Remove the lemon peel and clove and pour the jelly into warm, sterilised jars.

Cover and store in a cool place.

RASPBERRY JAM

Makes about 4-5 lbs
(1.75-2.25 kg)

The area around Dundee on the east coast is well-known for its raspberries.

3 lbs (1.5 kg) raspberries
3 lbs (1.5 kg) granulated sugar

Thoroughly wash the raspberries and put them into a preserving pan or a large saucepan.

Cook very gently over a low heat for about 10 minutes.

Warm the sugar and add to the fruit stirring until the sugar has dissolved.

Bring rapidly to the boil and boil for 2 minutes only then remove from the heat.

Pour the jam into dry, warm jars.

Place a circle of greaseproof paper over the jam and seal when cold.

DUNDEE MARMALADE

Makes about 6 lbs
(2.75 kg)

Dundee is famous for its marmalade. It began as a preserve made from quinces and takes its name from the Portuguese word for quince — 'marmelo'. Seville oranges in the preserve were substituted for the quinces and this new preserve quickly gained in popularity.

2 lbs (1 kg) Seville oranges
Juice and pips of 3 lemons
4 pints (2.25 litres/10 cups) water
4 lbs (1.75 kg) sugar

Wash the oranges thoroughly and cut into thin slices.

Put the slices into a large preserving pan with the water.

Bring to the boil and boil for about 1 hour.

Remove from the heat and allow to cool enough to be able to handle the oranges.

Remove the fruit and cut the rind into thin strips.

Remove the pips and put into a muslin bag with the pips from the lemons.

Return the orange pulp, the rind and the pips in the muslin bag to the preserving pan.

Add the lemon juice.

Bring to the boil again and boil rapidly for 15 minutes.

Remove the muslin bag of pips.

Warm the sugar and add to the mixture in the pan.

Stir over a low heat until the sugar has dissolved.

Bring to the boil and boil rapidly until setting point has been reached. This will be at 220°F/105°C when measured with a sugar thermometer. The mixture should set when a little is put on a cold saucer.

Leave the marmalade to cool a little then pour into hot, sterilised jars and seal.

TABLET

Tablet is another name for the fudge made in the Scottish Lowlands.

½ pint (300 ml/1¼ cups) milk
1 lb (450 g) granulated sugar
4 oz (100 g) butter
A few drops of vanilla essence

Put the milk and sugar into a large saucepan and heat gently until the sugar has dissolved.

Bring to the boil and boil rapidly until the mixure forms a soft ball when a little is dropped into cold water. This should take about 20 minutes.

Remove from the heat and add the butter and a few drops of vanilla essence.

Beat the mixture until the butter has melted and the mixture begins to set.

Pour into a greased and lined 7 inch (18 cm) square tin and leave to cool.

Cut into squares when cold and store in an airtight tin.

BUTTERSCOTCH

Makes 1 lb (450 g)

1 lb (450 g) demerara sugar
4 oz (100 g) butter
¼ pint (150 ml/⅔ cup) water
Juice of ½ lemon

Put the sugar, butter, water and lemon juice into a saucepan.

Heat gently until the sugar has dissolved and the butter has melted.

Bring to the boil and simmer, stirring all the time, for about 15 to 20 minutes until a teaspoonful of the mixture will harden when dropped into a cup of cold water.

Remove from the heat and beat vigorously for a few minutes.

Pour into a greased tin and leave to thicken.

Mark the surface into squares and leave to get cold.

When cold and set, break the butterscotch along the marks.

GLASGOW TOFFEE

Glaswegians were fond of making sweets in the 18th and 19th centuries as sugar was readily available, imported from the West Indies. The women who made these sweets and then sold them on the streets were named 'Sweety Wives'.

4 oz (100 g) butter
8 oz (225 g) sugar
¼ pint (150 ml/⅔ cup) milk
6 oz (175 g) golden syrup
2 oz (50 g) plain chocolate
A few drops of vanilla essence

Melt the butter in a saucepan.

Add the sugar, milk, golden syrup and pieces of chocolate.

Stir the mixture over a low heat until the sugar and syrup have dissolved.

Bring to the boil and boil rapidly til the point when the toffee will harden when a little is put into a cup of cold water. The temperature should reach 250°F/120°C.

Take off the heat and leave for a few minutes to cool slightly.

Beat in the vanilla essence and pour the toffee into a greased shallow tin.

Leave until the toffee has almost set then cut into squares.

The toffee should be wrapped in wax paper and kept in an airtight tin.

EDINBURGH ROCK

This is a well-known confection thought to have been first made by a young man called Sandy Ferguson who enjoyed making sweets in his own home. His sweets were so popular with his friends that he decided to go to Edinburgh to start making them on a larger scale. The rock is still made in Edinburgh from the original recipe.

1 lb (450 g) granulated sugar
7 fl oz (200 ml/¾ cup) water
½ teaspoon cream of tartar
Colouring and flavouring as desired
Icing sugar

Dissolve the sugar in the water over a low heat.

Add the cream of tartar.

Bring to the boil and boil rapidly until the temperature reaches 260°F/130°C or until the mixture forms a hard ball when a little is dropped into cold water.

Remove from the heat and stir in any flavouring and colouring.

When the mixture is cool enough to handle pour it on to an oiled surface.

Turn the edges of the mixture into the centre with an oiled knife.

When it becomes firm enough, sprinkle icing sugar over and pull the mixture up with your hands then let it drop down again. Continue in this way until the mixture hardens.

Pull into one long length about ½ inch (1 cm) thick then cut into shorter lengths.

Put these on tray dusted with icing sugar and sprinkle more icing sugar over the rock.

Leave in a warm place until the rock becomes powdery and crumbly. This may take anything from 1 to 7 days.

Store in an airtight tin.

WHIPKULL

Also known as Whipcol, this drink is traditionally served at Christmas breakfast in the Shetland Islands, a custom shared with the Norwegians.

4 oz (100 g) caster sugar
4 egg yolks
2 fl oz (3 tablespoons/¼ cup) rum

Put the sugar and the egg yolks in the top of a double boiler.

Beat over boiling water until the mixture is thick and creamy and the whisk leaves a trail.

Gradually add the rum, beating all the time.

Whisk for a further 5-10 minutes then pour into glasses.

This drink may be served hot or chilled and is especially good accompanied by rich shortbread.

GLASGOW PUNCH

Serves 4

This recipe dates back to the last century, if not longer. Rum was imported from the West Indies at this time.

Grated rind and juice of 1 orange
Grated rind and juice of 1 lemon
8 fl oz (250 ml/ 1 cup) dark rum
1¼ pints (750 ml/3 cups) water
4 oz (100 g) caster sugar

Mix the grated rind from the orange and lemon into the rum and leave for 24 hours.

Strain the liquid and reserve the rum.

Put the water and the sugar into a large saucepan.

Bring to the boil and boil rapidly without a lid until the mixture has been reduced to a little more than half.

Remove from the heat and leave to cool.

Stir in the orange and lemon juice and the rum.

Serve hot.

ATHOLL BROSE

Makes about 1 pint
(600 ml/2½ cups)

This creamy drink is named after the Duke of Atholl who lived in the 15th century and is believed to have enjoyed it. It is served on St. Andrew's Day and at Hogmanay.

2 oz (50 g) fine oatmeal
2 tablespoons clear heather honey
¼ pint (150 ml/⅔ cup) Scotch whisky
½ pint (300 ml/1¼ cups) water
¼ pint (150 ml/⅔ cup) single cream
1 teaspoon lemon juice

Mix the oatmeal and the water together, stir and leave for at least 1 hour.

Strain the liquid and discard the oatmeal.

Stir the honey into the liquid and heat gently until the honey has dissolved.

Remove from the heat and stir in the whisky and lemon juice.

Add the cream and whisk lightly to blend well.

Chill until needed.

SCOTTISH MILK

Serves 4

2 eggs
½ pint (300 ml/1¼ cups) milk
2 oz (50 g) caster sugar
4 tablespoons Scotch whisky
A little grated nutmeg

Separate the yolks of the eggs from the whites.

Beat the egg yolks with the sugar until thick.

Add the milk and whisky and whisk well.

Whisk the egg whites until stiff but not dry and fold into the drink.

Sprinkle with a little grated nutmeg.

Serve in chilled glasses.

THE COUNTRY RECIPE SERIES

Available now @ £1.95 each

Cambridgeshire
Cornwall
Cumberland & Westmorland
Derbyshire
Devon
Dorset
Gloucestershire
Hampshire
Kent
Lancashire
Leicestershire
Norfolk
Northumberland & Durham
Oxfordshire
Somerset
Suffolk
Sussex
Warwickshire
Wiltshire
Yorkshire

All these books are available at your local bookshop or newsagent, or can be ordered direct from the publisher. Just tick the titles you require and fill in the form below. Prices and availability subject to change without notice.

Ravette Books Limited, 3 Glenside Estate, Star Road, Partridge Green Horsham, West Sussex RH13 8RA.

Please send a cheque or postal order, and allow the following for postage and packing. UK 25p for one book and 10p for each additional book ordered.

Name ....

Address ....

....

....